The Effective EDP Manager

MICHAEL R. FRANK

amacom

A Division of
AMERICAN MANAGEMENT ASSOCIATIONS

The Effective EDP Manager

MICHAEL R. FRANK

amacom

A Division of

AMERICAN MANAGEMENT ASSOCIATIONS

Library of Congress Cataloging in Publication Data

Frank, Michael R
  The effective EDP manager.

  Includes index.
  1. Electronic data processing departments——Management.
I. Title.
HF5548.2.F725   658'.054   80-65876
ISBN 0-8144-5635-9

© 1980 AMACOM
A division of American Management Associations, New York.
All rights reserved. Printed in the United States of America.

FIRST PRINTING

Dedication

To all those who have struggled to control this organization resource of unbounded capacity and potential, and who have sometimes viewed this resource as one with equally monstrous capabilities.

Preface

This is a book about data processing. It is also a book about management. The underlying assumption is that despite phenomenal accomplishments, commercial EDP organizations on the whole have not lived up to the potential that technology provides. The basic theme here is that effective management techniques are needed to close the gap between potential and performance. Too often in the past, technology alone has been the solution to EDP problems, and sometimes technology itself has been an end.

EDP is an integral part of the business organization and as such is merely one of the tools of the organization, although clearly a very important one. EDP managers must understand the needs of the business and make their departments or groups responsive to those needs. Their objectives must be supportive of the business objectives, not ends in themselves. In order to accomplish this, EDP managers must acquire or improve their basic management skills, adapt them to fit their particular environment, and rely primarily on those skills to manage the EDP department.

An extremely important subtheme of the book is that EDP decisions require a long-range view. Major hardware and software commitments in fact represent capital acquisitions for the company. As with any major capital acquisition, long-range considerations are an absolute necessity when choosing direction.

The Effective EDP Manager is unique in approach. Although some conceptual discussion is required, the book is basically solution-oriented. It attempts to prescribe practical approaches to all the important areas of EDP management. The book provides "real world" insight into the approaches that will be successful, their justification, and some practical questions not normally addressed in this type of work.

Chapter 1 sets the stage for the presentation by reviewing the recent history, current status, and future of EDP organizations. Chapters 2 and 3 deal with the responsibilities of various executives with respect to EDP management and define a practical, efficient organization structure for the EDP department. Vital control techniques required in the EDP department are discussed in Chapters 4 through 6, followed by a presentation of issues and techniques of managing the critical human and hardware resources in Chapters 7 and 8. Planning, the indispensable foundation of the EDP organization, is discussed in Chapter 9 in a way that provides a starting point for the EDP manager. Chapter 10 offers a scheme for measuring performance once the basic tools are in place. Chapters 11 and 12 digress to several issues normally not addressed, but which inevitably will be encountered in the EDP environment and possibly may be vital to its success.

The book is written primarily for the data processing professional. More specifically, it is intended for professionals with EDP management responsibility or those who aspire to some day assume this responsibility. It also offers insight for the company executive who has direct EDP responsibility or who is indirectly—say, through committee participation—required to make EDP decisions. Students in both management and computer science curricula will benefit from this book. Any manager in today's environment must know how to deal with EDP, and the computer science major must broaden his area of expertise beyond technical areas.

The book is certainly not intended as an indictment of EDP managers. To the contrary, it recognizes the remarkable technology before us, the vast achievements made to date, and the far-reaching impact of computers in the future. Its perspective is that EDP managers have erred in the past, sometimes gravely, and must emphasize alternative approaches in the future if their organizations are to reach their full potential. Although no dramatically new concepts are offered, the techniques discussed should result in an improved data processing function.

MICHAEL R. FRANK

Contents

-1-
The EDP Mission

SIMPLY STATED, the EDP organization provides computer processing and related services. EDP organizations differ in character depending on specific circumstances, and range in nature from a small batch center to a large sophisticated state-of-the-art installation. In some, the cost control motive is predominant; in others, maintaining advanced technology is the highest priority. To effectively utilize the EDP resource, management must establish a goal, or guiding philosophy, upon which to base specific objectives, programs, and ongoing policy decisions. Because of the impact of the EDP function on the total organization, service is certainly an important consideration in goal determination. The significant expenditures associated with the EDP function require cost control as another major element.

But cost control and service are often in conflict. Does service mean providing the user with every application function requested? Does it make sense to strive for zero-defects quality? Is the least costly alternative always the best alternative? Is it reasonable to establish a limit for the EDP budget without consideration of other organizational requirements? Is minimizing today's cost for meeting today's service needs the necessary compromise? The answer to each of these questions is no.

The effective EDP organization develops only those applications which are justifiable in respect to costs and business needs. It provides an ongoing processing service that obtains and maintains

1

high standards of quality. It completes these activities in the most cost-effective way. Given the ever changing environment in both EDP and the business, it continues to build a capability for the future. In summary, the goal of the effective EDP organization can be stated as follows: *Provide cost-effective EDP services of high quality while providing for future needs and minimizing operating costs.*

RECENT HISTORY

In the 1960s, when EDP technology began to take giant steps forward, the EDP myth evolved. Essentially, the EDP myth was that this was a highly technical area understandable by only a few individuals, and therefore not adaptable to management techniques that had been successfully used in other functions. Because of the myth, executives sat back in dismay, witnessing one operational crisis after another while costs skyrocketed. They knew that this resource had great potential, and some even perceived it as the only salvation for some of their operating problems. So they waited and resigned themselves to the pain of the operation, but often wondered if the cure wasn't worse than the disease.

By the early 1970s the EDP myth was supposed to have been eradicated. Organizations began to recognize that the failure was not technical, but was in fact a failure to use proven management techniques. It was recognized that capable people in other parts of the organization could learn EDP technology and techniques. The EDP function was on the road to recovery. And surely the performance of many EDP departments did improve. New applications were developed that provided enormous benefits to the rest of the organization. Costs, with the help of technological advances, began to come under control. Expectations became more optimistic.

TODAY'S PROBLEM

But something is still wrong. Executives and user management are not always sure that the right applications are being developed, or at least in the right order. The data center doesn't always seem in

2

control of processing. Conversions are still painful. And cost and schedule overruns on new projects are often startling. Can this really be the nature of the beast? It certainly is not. Obviously, both operating and strategic errors will be made from time to time, but if this is the general situation, it is time for a reappraisal. The myth of the 1960s still lives on in too many organizations.

Mysterious technical explanations are offered and accepted for something that happened that wasn't wanted and for things that didn't happen that were wanted. Executives mutter to themselves, but go along with arguments that conversions never go really well because of the highly complex nature of the tasks. They are asked to take solace that this conversion was "trouble-free compared to what happened to another company." Chaos at month-end is merely a function of peak volumes. And because no two applications are exactly the same, it is impossible to accurately project budgets and schedules for development projects (although errors always turn out to be ones of understatement). The time has come to challenge these and similar arguments and eradicate the EDP myth once and for all.

If man can launch a rocket to the moon successfully, he can convert a computer system successfully. If large manufacturing plants can produce their products on schedule, a data center can deliver its reports on time. And most certainly, if a sophisticated strategic military weapon system can be developed on schedule and within budget, so can an EDP system.

Success in this context is a matter of deciding that success is the objective, assembling the right people and other resources, and managing the effort properly. To manage properly, those responsible must define strategies and objectives, outline the activities to be undertaken, plan how each task will be completed, monitor the progress, evaluate performance, and make adjustments as necessary. Within reason, management must make demands of the EDP function in two ways. First, it must establish high performance objectives. Second, it must establish an environment wherein nothing other than the achievement of these objectives is acceptable. Once these objectives are established, only a proper management approach will be successful in the long run in reaching them.

THE FUTURE

The future will bring greater challenges to EDP management. There seems to be no end to the expansion of EDP technology, and it continues to grow at an increasing rate. Technology provides many new opportunities, but its increasing complexity also increases the difficulty of management. Size alone—and EDP departments do grow—requires more skilled management. And perhaps most important, as more EDP applications are developed, making the EDP department even more critical to the success of the business, the requirements for reliability and accuracy will be even more demanding. Technology is already growing at a rate greater than businesses' ability to assimilate it. And business objectives are already making demands for quality faster than EDP departments can meet them. So change is necessary now.

-2-
The Managers of Data Processing

A REFERENCE to the managers of data processing is usually meant to include the director of data processing, possibly the systems manager or the computer operations manager, or even lower-echelon functional managers. The corporate president, the vice president of finance, and other executives are not normally thought of as managers of data processing, although, in fact, any executive responsible for data processing within his or her organization is a manager of data processing.

To some, this may sound so obvious as to seem trivial. But, in a preponderance of organizations, top executives do not actively and meaningfully participate in the management of the EDP function. Some executives review development schedules and priorities and make judgments regarding capital expenditures. Others don't even participate to this level. They abdicate responsibility under the pretense of "trusting the experts." This saves time and helps them avoid the task of developing a working understanding of this function. A top executive would probably never agree to a change in market tactics, production schedules, or personnel policy without understanding the reasoning behind these proposals; yet major decisions are made in the EDP department without his knowledge. Effective executives challenge inaction in many areas of the organization and even initiate programs and policies; yet they may let EDP roll along its own way.

5

THE LACK OF TOP MANAGEMENT PARTICIPATION

Why aren't more top executives more active in EDP management? First, they probably don't know anything about EDP and are not comfortable with it. Also, participation requires time. Burdened with many strategic problems, the executive finds it difficult to budget substantial time for this function. Many top managers don't recognize the importance of the EDP function within their organization. Finally, often the EDP manager will subtly discourage active participation of top executives. "Let me give you the bottom line so this won't take too much time." "These assumptions are based on a highly technical analysis, which we will not bore you with." Attitudes like these, well-intentioned or not, deprive top executives of the opportunity to really understand the basis of important decisions.

The last argument for the lack of participation of executives is presented as "That's what we pay the director of EDP to do." But this is no more defensible than leaving marketing strategy totally to the vice president of marketing or the financial decisions strictly to the vice president of finance. The top executive has the right and the responsibility to ensure that strategically the EDP function, like every other function, moves in the direction his judgment deems best. Even though the director of data processing may well be a top-notch manager, he probably won't provide the most imaginative and effective leadership if he is left unchallenged. No one performs to his peak in the long run if he is not challenged periodically. Also, the top executive must protect the organization from the EDP manager who is not fully competent or lacks commitment. Too often, deficiencies are not recognized until the performance of the EDP department slips to the point that it engulfs the entire organization in crisis.

In many organizations, the EDP budget is a significant part of the total operating costs. Many key departments are totally dependent on the EDP department. And often top management, in making major decisions, relies on EDP as virtually its entire source of information on the business. These facts make the EDP department an unquestionably vital function, and its importance will continue to increase. Therefore, top management must become much more involved. What are the steps they must take to make this happen?

EDUCATING THE TOP EXECUTIVE

The executive must first educate himself in respect to data processing. The typical top executive may have been through one or more of the chairs of marketing, finance, or manufacturing, but chances are he has never been associated with data processing other than in the role of a user. And he most likely wasn't too active in this capacity. So, he probably needs to begin with basics.

There are many sources for this education. Some vendors provide excellent executive seminars, although the participant must recognize that these presentations may include some prejudiced views and will probably contain certain subtle marketing points. Participating in a seminar provided by one or more vendors competitive to the installation may be both interesting and informative. Also, both professional associations and other private companies provide educational programs. There are many useful books and magazine articles. The in-house experts can be a valuable source of information. Formal presentations on specific subject areas by the EDP staff provide not only general education but also insights on how the EDP department of the organization is run. Informal discussions with the EDP manager on certain technical and policy areas are a learning experience and will help the executive get to know the EDP manager and his abilities better. On an ongoing basis, the in-house discussions will continue to keep top management abreast of EDP trends. The executive should also continue participation in seminars to understand new technology and to develop a deeper understanding of EDP. Skimming through EDP periodicals will help the top executive keep up to date on major new developments in the field.

As with any major function within the organization, the more the top executive knows about EDP, the better off he is. But one must be practical about personal time limitations and outline a program that is realistic. If this endeavor is not presented in a threatening

7

manner, the EDP manager can probably be the best consultant in providing assistance. Two general checklists of areas of knowledge the top executive should acquire follow. These are segregated into two areas: technology and techniques. Knowledge of technology refers to the understanding of the computer system, its components and technical considerations regarding its use. Techniques are concerned with the procedures that surround the use of the computer technology. This book does not address the technical areas, other than in the broadest sense. Subsequent chapters will discuss data processing techniques in considerable detail.

EDP Skills for the Top Executive: Technology

Hardware Architecture
  CPU Function
  Peripheral Types
  Interaction of System
    Configuration
Systems Software
  Types
  Functions
  Maintenance Considerations
Programming Languages
  Principal Languages
  Capability of Each Language
Hardware Alternatives
  Important Vendors
  Plug-Compatibles
  Configuration Issues

Communication Systems
  Application Justification
  Network Architecture
  Communications Software
  Terminal Alternatives
Data Base Systems
  Data Base Philosophy
  Data Base Software
  Data Base Impact on Systems
    Development
Hardware Capacity Considerations
  Determining Utilization
  Limiting Factors
  Migration Considerations

EDP Skills for the Top Executive: Techniques

EDP Organizational Considerations
Systems Operations
  Project Development Methods
  Project Control Techniques
  Quality Assurance Methods
Computer Operations
  Scheduling Procedures
  Input/Output Control
  Data File Control
Management of Change

Personnel Management in the EDP
  Labor Market
Performance Measurement
  Key Measurement Criteria
  Interpreting Reports
EDP Documentation Requirements
Security
  Physical Access
  Data Protection

8

The obvious question in respect to these checklists is how much the executive must in fact know. To repeat, as with any other function in the organization, the more he knows and understands, the better off he is. The objective of the top executive is to direct EDP, review the decisions of EDP management, challenge its policies, and measure its performance. These activities require a fairly in-depth understanding. A basic understanding of hardware components, functions, and capacity is absolutely essential. The purpose of systems software and user/vendor relationships are important areas seldom addressed. The top executive should know what programming languages are available, what their capabilities are, what advantages and disadvantages each has, and in what situation each is best used. Because of the costs and the growing importance of data base and data communication systems, the top manager should have a thorough understanding of the concepts of each and know to what type of application systems each applies. The techniques listed in the second checklist may not be very technical, but they require considerable depth of knowledge. A sound working knowledge of EDP technique is required in order to evaluate recommendations, analyze problems, and generally make judgments about the performance of the EDP function. Without an understanding of the tools available, it is difficult to quantify expectations.

THE ROLE OF TOP EXECUTIVES

To ensure his participation, the executive must place the EDP function organizationally at a level that allows him access to it. The EDP function is of much greater significance than a small operational department and should not be buried in the organization at a similar level. Specifics regarding organization structure are discussed at length in Chapter 3.

An important responsibility of any top executive is the development of intermediate- and long-range plans. The executive must carry out this responsibility at the company level, involve the director of data processing in the process, and ensure that long-range plans are developed for the EDP department. Today's application systems tend to be extensive in scope, and development lead times are substantial. Therefore, the further in advance an EDP manager knows of a requirement, the easier it is to ensure orderly development and quality systems. Crash projects contrived by shortsighted top management inevitably increase costs, hurt morale, and tempt a catastrophe. Also, hardware and software migration plans and financial decisions such as lease versus buy are made intelligently only when insight into the future is a consideration. The data processing manager must be considered a key member of the management team privy to the organization's secrets.

The top executive must participate in the important decisions regarding EDP. He should be active in deciding on major hardware acquisitions, setting systems software and other technical strategies, making major application decisions (including application priorities), and determining resource allocation. He should also be aware of the general performance in the operating environment.

By way of clarification, it is beneficial to enumerate some items the top executive should stay out of. The data processing manager should manage his people. The top executive should not try to influence personnel assignments or evaluate personnel, and he should give his subordinates a certain latitude in organization structure. Purely technical considerations like program design can only be confused by the executive's presence. Unnecessary intervention in daily priorities can unnecessarily bog down operational management and can sometimes have devastating results if done with limited knowledge. There is no exhaustive checklist of do's and don'ts. Again, the top executive must approach data processing as he does other important functions in the organization. He must direct EDP, but he must not overmanage. He must exercise good judgement based on his understanding of the function and according to the circumstances.

Executive management must monitor and evaluate the performance of the EDP function on a continuous basis. Reacting to crises or responding to problems reported by other departments is not adequate. The monitoring activity is another reason for the executive to understand the function. If he doesn't know how it operates,

10

he doesn't even know what to measure. Based on the top executive's understanding of the function, he should establish a comprehensive reporting program. There are many measurement tools available.

To manage any function, management should develop a plan and a supporting budget for the function. This should include specific performance objectives for the period, as well as supporting programs. An analysis of performance against this plan is essential to the evaluation of EDP or any other organizational unit. But, in the short run this analysis can camouflage hidden problems. Other key operating statistics must be reviewed regularly.

Results of development projects in terms of budgets and schedules are vital data. The extent of operational disruptions resulting from conversions should be understood. Summary level indicators, such as percentages of on-time user deliveries and the quality of reports, can also be useful. Internal and external audits, when performed well, can give good evaluations of control and security. Approached properly and structured well, a periodic operations review by a competent consulting firm can provide beneficial recommendations for EDP and top management.

Of course, the performance appraisal of the EDP manager himself is vital. A results-against-objectives evaluation is the basis of this. But evaluation must go a step further, because there is a fallacy in the measurement-by-objectives approach. An inept manager, if supported by capable subordinates, can be successful in the short run. The specific contributions of the data processing manager should be noted. One should suspect a manager who constantly must check with a subordinate to answer a question or who always appears at a meeting with a supporting cast of assistants.

To many, the preceding remarks will be shocking. The actions suggested will be labeled time-consuming and unnecessary for executives. But if top management restricts its role to superficial reviews, real problems will not be identified until crisis proportions are reached. A thorough evaluation by top management is a plus for the capable EDP manager, too, because it can highlight his real performance and his value to the organization. All too often, his only tribute is absence of complaint.

11

The last and most important role of the top executive is his selection of the EDP manager. This decision will be the most important one for the top executive in relation to data processing. Notwithstanding our emphasis, in this chapter, on the importance of top management involvement, the EDP manager is the most vital element in the successful EDP organization. The top executive must clearly understand the requirements for this position and select the best candidate available to fill it. His screening must be both skillful and thorough. A mistake can literally bring disastrous results.

QUALIFICATIONS OF THE DIRECTOR OF DATA PROCESSING

In many respects, the director of data processing has one of the most demanding positions in the organization. Few other managers of highly technical areas have such extensive resources to direct. And few managers of functions of comparable size must deal with so many issues of such technical complexity. Clearly, EDP management, regardless of the size of the organization, is not a one-man show, but the EDP manager sets the climate in the EDP organization and determines its basic character. His responsibility of choosing key subordinates alone will be fundamental to the performance of the department.

What kind of people are suitable to such responsibilities? First of all, they are businesspeople. They understand the business objectives of the organization and consider the impact of their decisions and recommendations on those objectives. They are managers in every sense of the word and are especially skillful at monitoring and controlling a large number of projects, problems, and issues simultaneously. They must have the inclination and ability to deal in highly technical planning and problem solving. They must be able to present themselves well to all levels of management, both inside and outside the organization, and to deal effectively in all of these situations. To be successful, they must be skillful at directing others. And they must thrive on a high-pressure environment and a fast-paced job. They must acquire a knowledge of the business and its industry, and preferably of other industries. And they must under-

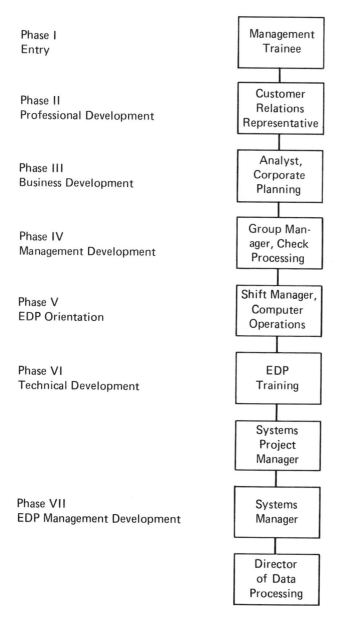

Phase I Entry	Management Trainee
Phase II Professional Development	Customer Relations Representative
Phase III Business Development	Analyst, Corporate Planning
Phase IV Management Development	Group Man- ager, Check Processing
Phase V EDP Orientation	Shift Manager, Computer Operations
Phase VI Technical Development	EDP Training
	Systems Project Manager
Phase VII EDP Management Development	Systems Manager
	Director of Data Processing

Figure 2-1. Ideal career path to EDP manager in banking.

13

stand the basics of EDP technology or have the ability to quickly assimilate them.

RECRUITING THE EDP MANAGER

Ideally, the EDP manager should come from within the organization and have developed his skills from within the organization. Figure 2-1 depicts a nearly ideal career path for an EDP manager within a bank as an example. It is illustrative of the type of movement his career should take to ensure the right development. This process would take several years, but, with the right candidate, should yield an excellent individual for the EDP manager's position. Paths will differ depending on the nature and needs of each organization.

Inside development has the advantage of providing a manager who knows the organization, has a stake in it, and has a proven record. Sometimes, this approach is not feasible for a number of reasons, and an EDP manager must be recruited from the outside. This recruiting project should be carefully thought out. The best candidate for the position is a proven director of data processing from another company. Industry experience is useful but not a necessity if the candidate meets the other requirements. The problem with this is that successful EDP managers often seek to change companies in order to improve their career. Therefore, it may be necessary to provide a plan of additional responsibilities in a relatively short period. This decision must be made on an individual basis according to the circumstances. Caution should be exercised when interviewing an experienced manager who is willing to make a lateral move. A hidden problem may be present.

After considering experienced EDP managers, the candidates from the next lower echelon of EDP managers should be considered. A second-level manager in a larger organization might be an excellent candidate. The systems manager is the candidate with the highest probability of success. The computer operations manager may be considered, but often he or she does not have the technical background to work effectively with the total responsibility.

14

Regardless of the source, the potential manager must be screened carefully. If no current EDP manager is present to participate in the interviewing, outside assistance may well be required to make a technical evaluation. The EDP manager is in fact a key executive. This should be remembered in determining compensation and rank. As alluded to earlier, occasionally an especially bright and aggressive individual with proven management credentials in another area of the organization can make the transition and assume the responsibilities of the EDP manager. But it takes an especially capable person to quickly grasp the technology and gain the respect of subordinates.

RESPONSIBILITIES OF THE EDP MANAGER

Once in his position, the manager or director of data processing should be responsible for the direction and performance of the EDP function. He should have the primary responsibility for the development of the EDP plan and budget and be accountable for execution of these. Selection of subordinate personnel should be his responsibility, and he must answer for the overall performance of his staff. The director of data processing should also be expected to maintain an organization structure appropriate to the environment, provide the most cost-effective hardware configuration, and ensure a data center operation that offers users top-quality service and a well-controlled environment. Also, the director of data processing, through knowledge of the business and developments in other parts of the industry, should recommend innovative ways to use the computer to enhance the performance of the overall organization. As discussed in detail earlier in this chapter, other executives should participate in many of these areas, but the director of data processing should be primarily accountable for all those areas that are fundamental to the effective data processing organization.

In order to accomplish his objectives, the director of data processing must have broad authority. Given the limits of review and justification, he must retain freedom in day-to-day operations. He has to be allowed access to top executives in the corporation so that he can obtain the information he requires. He must have the power to hire, terminate, promote, and set salary levels for data processing personnel. He should have complete access to vendors and be relatively unencumbered by traditional purchasing functions. And within the guidelines of the approved plan, he requires a certain latitude in relation to modifications to the plan, provided they do not substantially disrupt the basic strategy encompassed by the plan.

Because of the broad scope of his position, the director of data processing must be ever cautious to ensure that he does not become so involved in any one or a few problems that he loses control of the organization. This is a danger that any top manager must avoid, but the data processing manager is especially susceptible to it because of the large number of activities typical of his organization and the volatile nature of the environment.

The director of data processing must act as the moving force in the EDP department. He must direct his organization according to the established plan, coordinate interrelated activities, and review progress of subordinates. He should solve problems of a strategic nature and leave technical problem solving to the people responsible. During a major disruption, the director of data processing may have to convene the appropriate individuals to review the problem-solving plan and ensure a coordinated effort. But he must refuse to debug programs or diagnose hardware malfunctions, regardless of how skillful he thinks he might be in one of these areas. If the director of data processing finds himself repeatedly drawn into these activities, he must either question the skills of his staff or suspect that he has made an overinflated appraisal of his own contributions.

Delegation obviously is important in a large organization. But even in the smallest installations, someone must fill the management role. If the data processing manager is looked upon only as a programmer with the title, the potential of the organization will never be reached. Certainly, in the smallest EDP departments, a full-time manager may not be cost-effective, but someone must assume the management responsibility as the top-priority activity among all other duties.

To run a really effective EDP organization, the EDP manager must provide a talented, well-motivated staff. This staff must be properly organized and provided the proper tools to successfully perform the jobs. Now that the criteria for the top managers of EDP have been established, the remaining chapters will deal with the development of EDP structures and techniques.

-3-
EDP
Organization

THE DEVELOPMENT of the EDP organization structure requires three related but distinct steps. All three of these steps must be completed if the EDP function is to work effectively. In addition, because the EDP environment is dynamic, the EDP organization must undergo constant review and change to adapt to the evolving requirements. The proper organization structure is the one that is most effective, at the time, in letting the EDP carry out its responsibilities and activities.

EDP'S PLACE IN THE COMPANY

The first consideration in EDP organization is to whom the director of EDP (and thereby the entire EDP organization) will report. This is a decision made casually in some organizations, and often by the accident of circumstances, but it can be very important to the long-term effectiveness of the function. In many companies, EDP reports to the controller or financial officer. This may have resulted from the acquisition of the original computer as an accounting device or a notion that this structure would emphasize cost control. Banks often place EDP within an operating division with functions such as check processing only for a lack of a better place. This assignment has some serious drawbacks.

18

When the EDP director reports to a controller or a bank operations officer, he may be unduly influenced in prioritizing resources in favor of the functions within the division to which he belongs. This leaves the other users struggling for required services. Granted, active executive officers can control priorities in respect to the overall business needs, but this organization can lead to problem situations. More important, when EDP reports to a function that is a major user, it can lose some of its objectivity. It is difficult to recommend not to proceed with a project that might be the boss's pet. EDP has the clear responsibility to evaluate requests from users and to recommend improved methods for the business. It cannot freely exercise these responsibilities when it is not independent.

As discussed in Chapter 2, EDP must be placed high enough in the organization to be effective. Its relative importance and impact on the business must be reflected in the overall structure. Because of the great variety of structures within corporations and other organizations, precise prescriptions for the reporting relationships are difficult. But there are some general approaches to consider. EDP could effectively report to a general administration division with functions such as personnel, security, building management, and so on. Again, the important thing is that the other functions in the division should not be major users. Especially in organizations with very large EDP functions, it is often justifiable to place EDP on a divisional level and have it report directly to an executive officer. This decision must be carefully evaluated by top planners. Objectivity and independence must be the predominant criteria.

PRINCIPLES OF EDP ORGANIZATION

After the position of EDP relative to the rest of the business is determined, the second, and more complex, task is the design of the EDP structure. Throughout, the discussion has assumed the presence of a director of data processing. Many businesses have attempted to run their EDP functions without this position. Typical would be a structure built around a systems manager and an operations manager, both reporting to someone with other, non-EDP responsibilities. This type of structure is doomed to failure for a lack of coordination, the absence of one individual with the time and background to initiate a cohesive plan and direct the function accordingly, and the resultant interorganizational conflict. This alternative is so impractical that it is not even considered for serious discussion.

Assuming the presence of an EDP director, we must begin the organizational analysis with a review of principles common to all organization decisions. The structure is primarily based on the functions to be performed and the number of people performing them. The personnel must be sorted into groups according to functions, in a way that provides a clear-cut set of responsibilities and minimizes overlap and organizational conflict. At the same time, the organization should provide checks and balances. That is, a contention system should be used to bring organizational issues to the surface. Every individual should have only one boss, and the span of control of each management level should be carefully controlled. Mechanisms to coordinate related functions must be provided. Unnecessary management overhead such as one-on-one reporting relationships should be avoided. Staff support for operations should be used when beneficial from the standpoint of providing expertise and economies of scale, but it should not be allowed to usurp authority of line managers.

Some suggest that the structure not be built around people. They argue that the optimum organization should be implemented and people should be recruited to fit it. But in practice this is not realistic. The labor market for outstanding talent is limited, so there is a natural tendency (and good business justification) for setting up an organization that takes full advantage of the talents available and is suitable to some extent to the styles of these individuals. Also, the ideal organization might reasonably be altered to resolve unworkable personality situations or other staff conditions. The key to success is finding the proper balance. It is not feasible to develop a structure without consideration of the individuals involved; on the other hand, a structure established without due consideration of the principles discussed will fail. The proper approach is to first design

20

reporting relationships on the basis of evaluations of principles and develop a picture of the ideal situation. Then the structure should be considered with respect to individuals. Changes can be made after careful consideration of their importance and of their impact on the proposed approach.

In a function such as EDP, there are two conflicting performance requirements. Long-range planning and orderly development are a must. On the other hand, the department must be responsive to the service demands of problem solving and attending to new requirements. Attempts must be made through effective planning to minimize the occurrence of last-minute requirements, but these will never be eliminated. Reactions to unexpected competitive actions, regulatory changes, economic conditions, and scores of other external factors are a way of life in even the most well-managed companies. The EDP organization must recognize these conflicting demands by segregating resources for each purpose within the structure.

BASIC EDP FUNCTIONS

Any data processing organization, regardless of size, must provide three broad operating functions if it is to be effective. These are program development, computer processing, and technical development. In addition, there are several administrative and management functions vital to the EDP department. Table 3-1 lists these functional areas and the principal activities within each. The illustration is not intended to suggest any specific structure at this point, but only to provide a list of those functions that must be performed by someone.

The initial step in developing the organization is to review these functions and identify the issues that are important to structure. Regardless of the size of the EDP department, distinct computer processing and program development groups are a requirement. The questions usually arise in respect to the technical development function and the administrative and management function.

21

Table 3-1. Functions of the EDP organization.

FUNCTIONAL AREA	ACTIVITIES
Program development	Analyze potential systems and determine feasibility Design approved systems according to requirements of users Program systems Test and implement systems Maintain systems
Computer processing	Receive input and keypunch Maintain data files Process computer runs Dispatch output Maintain hardware
Technical development	Hardware analysis System software development and maintenance Data communications development (if applicable) Data base development (if applicable)
Administrative planning and budgeting	Long-range planning and budgeting Establish standards and procedures Design and administer security Provide recruiting assistance Conduct training

ISSUES OF FUNCTIONAL ORGANIZATION

The placement of the technical development functions varies greatly within EDP departments. In some, the functions are split between the group responsible for computer processing and the one responsible for program development. Hardware analysis usually becomes part of the computer processing function, and the remainder is associated with the program development function.

This split has several drawbacks. It does not recognize the importance of the relationship between hardware and systems software and the need for well-planned, coordinated development. Also, by making these activities add-on activities, they may not get the emphasis they deserve. Finally, this approach does not provide any functional checks and balances for the overall organization. Other companies consolidate the technical development functions into a separate group and assign it to either the program development or computer operations functions. This structure usually results in the technical development personnel aligning too closely with one of the groups at the expense of the other.

The optimum organization is one which provides for a separate group for the technical development function. This group is responsible for development of a consolidated hardware/system software plan, execution of the plan, and general technical support for the EDP department.

It should be noted that the hardware analysis activity is often an emotional issue. Data center managers will argue, with some merit, that because they have the responsibility for operating the computers, they should plan and configure the hardware. This was more plausible in the past, but with the complexity of today's configuration, these activities must be completed by people with the technical ability of the systems programmer found in a technical development group. Such people usually are not interested in being in a computer processing group. However, the computer processing staff's argument is one that should not be ignored. The computer processing group must be made a part of the process of developing the hardware plan. Also, the computer processing group must be protected from surprises such as the delivery of unexpected hardware. A good check and balance for this purpose is to require all orders to be placed by the computer processing group. This practice can also be a valuable control for the director of data processing. Because of the importance of the hardware responsibility, a thorough analysis is necessary. Table 3-2 is a summary of a workable distribution of hardware responsibilities.

Administrative functions must be provided in the organization. The placement of these functions, too, is sometimes received with an emotional reaction. The way these functions are structured is determined by the size of organization. The small department cannot justify individuals designated for these activities, while the larger installations cannot do without them. But regardless of the size of the department, these activities must be performed by someone.

In the smaller installation these activities are normally assumed by

Table 3-2. Recommended distribution of hardware responsibilities.

UNIT OR INDIVIDUAL	RESPONSIBILITIES
Top Management	Approve hardware changes as required.
Director of Data Processing	Approve all hardware changes. Monitor performance of subordinate groups.
Computer Processing Group	Place all hardware orders. Maintain records of all hardware installed and on order. Maintain facility and install hardware. Interact with vendor to maintain hardware. Review and comment on recommendations for changes.
Technical Development Group	Use sophisticated techniques and monitor hardware utilization and determine trends. Identify new hardware requirements and impact on utilization trends. Analyze new hardware offered by vendors. Provide detailed configuration changes. Recommend configuration changes.

the director of data processing and subordinate levels of management. In the larger installation, the situation is more complex. Often each of the managers of the three operating groups—computer processing, program development, and technical development—desires his own staff support to perform these functions. This structure gives them the advantage of control over their own functions. However, the proliferation of administrative staff probably increases the total cost, because economies of scale are not achieved and coordination problems arise, placing an additional burden on the director of data processing. For example, the planning function obviously needs a coordinated effort and some consolidation. Security policies and procedures also must encompass the total EDP department.

The larger EDP department should, therefore, define a staff group reporting to the director of data processing to perform these administrative activities. Ideally, the structure will include two groups: a planning and budgeting group and an administrative support group responsible for standards and procedures, security, recruiting, and training. The latter group could also assume any miscellaneous administrative functions such as requisitioning supplies, planning floor space, and taking care of various other duties as assigned by the director of data processing.

The staff groups support not only the director of data processing but the other EDP groups as well. If they are to be valuable to the entire EDP department, they must develop a service-oriented philosophy and be responsive to all users. The groups must provide quality support and clearly know the limits of their responsibilities and authority. They should never behave as superiors to the operating groups. The staff managers and the director of data processing must ensure that these guidelines are followed.

ESTABLISHING THE ORGANIZATION STRUCTURE

After identifying the functions of the EDP department, designating groups to complete the activities of each, and analyzing the organizational issues involved, it is possible to start developing the organization chart. Figures 3-1 and 3-2 depict the top-level organization for a small and a large organization, respectively. The activities defined in Table 3-1 are indicated under the designated groups. Group names have been altered from previous references to be consistent with common usage.

The most significant difference between the large department and the small one is the assignment of the activities relating to the administrative and management function and the resultant role of the director of data processing and the managers of each group. In the larger installation, the director of data processing has no functional activities assigned to him. He does have functional responsibilities in the smaller installations, as do subordinate managers. This does not mean that the operating managers do not participate in these activities in the larger organizations, but the primary responsibility for the development of methods lies with the support group.

25

Note that the hardware analysis activity appears in both the technical support and computer services groups. This is consistent with the previous analysis and detail in Table 3-2.

The size of "large" and "small" organizations has intentionally not been quantified. There are realistically many classifications of size, ranging from very small ones with no subordinate managers under the EDP manager to the supersize ones found in the federal government and large corporations. Figures 3-1 and 3-2 and the accompanying discussions are intended to provide guidelines, and the two examples demonstrate how organization changes as a func-

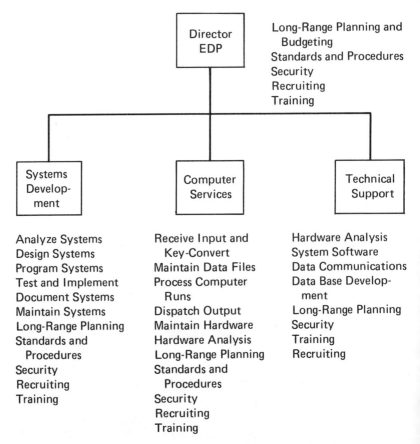

Figure 3-1.   Organization of a small EDP installation.

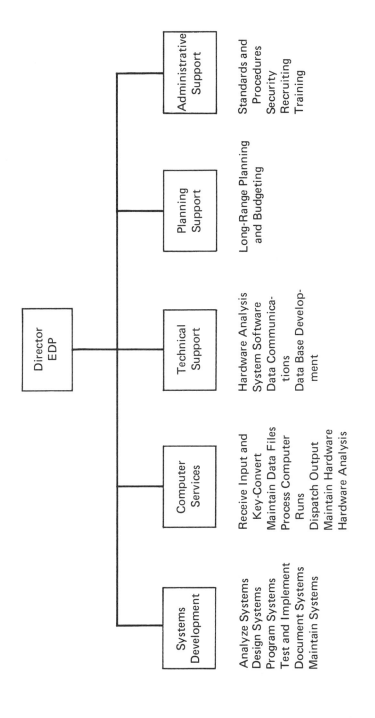

Figure 3-2. Organization of a large EDP installation.

tion of size. Determination of a specific structure must be a result of understanding the environment and making judgments according to the guidelines. Again, the important fact is that each of the activities identified must be provided for in every organization.

USER SERVICE FUNCTIONS

One activity of the EDP organization that has not been discussed is user contact and user relations. A review of this has intentionally been withheld pending the development of the basic structure. Given the overall nature of the EDP department and the importance of providing effective service, user contact is extremely important. By no means should this activity be left to happen at random as circumstances dictate. There must be a well thought-out arrangement, and all members of the EDP staff should be disciplined to

Table 3-3. Responsibility guidelines for user communication.

NATURE OF CONTACT	RESPONSIBILITY
Communications by EDP regarding its activities.	All levels of EDP management.
Requests by user for new systems.	Systems development manager.
Requests by users regarding systems modifications.	Systems development manager.
Discussions on the development or modification of systems.	Systems analyst assigned.
Users' reports of problems regarding timeliness, accuracy, or quality of reports.	Customer representative in the computer services group.
User requests for special runs.	Customer representative in the computer services group.
Service reviews.	Director of data processing; computer services manager; systems development manager.
Long-range planning.	Planning support manager.

abide by the guidelines. Users should also understand and follow procedures established.

Table 3-3 displays the type of contacts between the EDP and user departments and provides guidelines for who should be charged with handling the communication. This illustration is oriented toward a larger installation, but with an understanding of the principles involved, it can easily be applied to any EDP department.

All members of EDP management have a responsibility to communicate to users on EDP activities and to "sell" the department. This can be achieved on an informal basis as well as through a planned program. Requests for systems activity should be directed to the EDP manager so that he can control assignments and priorities. Obviously, the user must speak directly to computer services to request runs, and the planning support group will need to communicate with users too. But the designations of the other two activities may not be quite as clear.

Many EDP departments fail to provide users with a good vehicle to solve problems with production work received from computer services. Many users are forced to guess as to the cause of problems and then go to one or more individuals within the computer services group if they suspect an operating cause, or search out someone in systems development if a program bug is suspected. This setup is, of course, frustrating to the user. EDP also suffers from this practice, because often two or even more individuals end up working on the same problem.

The solution to this dilemma is to designate somebody in computer services as a customer representative. In a large data center, this may be one or more full-time people. In a smaller one, the activity may be assumed by the operations supervisor. This person should be responsible for receiving reports of problems, documenting them, making a determination of the nature of the problem, and passing them on to the appropriate individual, either in computer services or systems development, for resolution. Also, the customer representative should follow up on the progress of problem resolution, report status to users, and prepare appropriate management reports. This approach will ensure the best response to the user and the most efficient use of EDP resources.

The method for controlling problems will be discussed in a subsequent chapter, but one point is worthy of note at this time. Problem control requires individual documentation of each problem. This documentation should always be completed by the customer representative, not the user. The most infuriating thing any customer can encounter is to be told that in order to get a problem corrected, he must fill out a form.

User service reviews are an important part of the communication between the user and EDP. A formal program of service reviews is necessary to supplement daily informal communication. The user must be asked how he perceives the timeliness and quality of EDP products and the overall responsiveness of the EDP department. The systems development and computer services managers should conduct relevant interviews with the heads of the user departments. In some organizations where service reviews are conducted, the interviews are delegated to a lower level. This is better than nothing, but it has certain pitfalls. The individual interviewing cannot always speak for the group or department and may not have access to the user department head.

The director of data processing should also periodically conduct service reviews. He needs to have first-hand information on this important responsibility. This is a good check and balance, and the director probably has access to higher-level managers in user areas who can provide a different perspective.

ORGANIZATION OF THE
SYSTEMS DEVELOPMENT GROUP

At this point, the functions of the EDP department as a whole have been identified, the issues relative to its organization have been discussed, and the top-level structure of the EDP department has been determined. In order to complete the design of the EDP department organization, the same analysis must be completed for each group identified in the charts in either Figure 3-1 or Figure 3-2.

Systems development groups are organized in many different ways. Considerations regarding the structure of systems development groups are similar to those discussed in relation to the overall

EDP department. But there is a special aspect to the systems development organization because it must serve two masters. Systems development provides new computer applications as well as maintaining the current ones. The development activity requires thoughtful planning and skillful project management. Resources are committed to activities for long periods in the future. Effective maintenance support requires a highly responsive resource that can react to changes in priorities as quickly as circumstances change. If the systems development group is not structured properly, the two requirements can come into conflict.

With an inappropriate structure, maintenance requests can be pushed aside because of the pressures of meeting development schedule deadlines, thereby hindering customer service. On the other hand, peak maintenance loads can be disruptive to development schedules. Fundamentally, there are two ways to organize the systems development group. The first is to leave maintenance to the development personnel who wrote the application. The second is to assign maintenance to a section established for application maintenance of all systems. There are important arguments for each.

If all activity, including development and maintenance, is controlled by the same people, an expertise is obtained regarding that application. The user talks only to a few individuals about requirements. Sometimes resources can be better utilized because more personnel can be assigned to maintenance during peak periods; when maintenance is low, resources can be used in development activities. All changes to an application can be controlled by one person, and there is little risk of problems arising as a result of two programmers working on the same application at the same time.

Segregating maintenance into a separate section has several advantages too. Development projects are isolated from disruptions of maintenance activities. Maintenance response will in general probably be better. It is easier to coordinate mass changes affecting all applications required by a change in hardware configuration or systems software. Checks and balances are improved, because as the recipient and user of systems and program documentation, the maintenance section can be used as a reviewer of these products during the development cycle.

Either organization structure will work, and in fact does in many EDP departments. It is a matter of judgment which set of advantages carries the most weight. But no matter which solution is selected, procedures must be established to protect against its disadvantages. However, the organization with a separate maintenance section will be successful most often and more effective overall, because it protects development schedules and provides higher-quality maintenance service, thus best supporting the overall goal of the EDP department.

When implementing this structure, thoughtful evaluation must be given to the criteria for what constitutes a maintenance activity versus a development project. Certainly not all changes to an existing application should be considered maintenance, because some enhancements are so broad in scope as to require a major development project. On the other end of the spectrum, fixes to problems reported in calculation, report formats, and the like will always be maintenance. The question is where the line is drawn to separate the functions. This normally should be quantified in terms of estimated hours of completion. Tasks requiring more time than standard are development, and smaller ones are maintenance. This number will vary from installation to installation, depending on the size of the resource and the project load.

The size of the maintenance group is based on its history of activities. The group should be expected to grow as the application volume grows, and requirements will be greater in a state-of-the-art EDP department where frequent hardware and systems software changes are made. Because the development schedules are more stable and longer-range in time, it must be the maintenance section's responsibility to know when development enhancement projects are under way and to ensure that maintenance on a program basis is scheduled around these activities.

Figures 3-3 demonstrates the basic, simplified systems development group organization structure discussed so far. In the smaller installation this may in fact be the total structure. The maintenance section may be one person, and the development section could be three or four analyst/programmers working on one project with the systems development manager, who acts as project manager. Variations are countless as size increases. The larger the project volume,

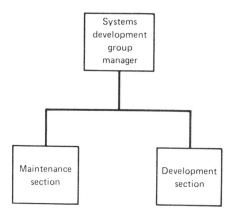

Figure 3-3. Basic organization of the systems development group.

the larger the systems development staff and the more complex the organization.

MORE COMPLEX
SYSTEMS DEVELOPMENT ORGANIZATIONS

Typically, in the larger shops there is a separation in the positions of systems analyst and programmer. This differentiation raises a question about the structure of the systems development group. One way to organize is to establish one group with programmers and one with systems analysts. The other is to organize on a project basis, with programmers and analysts within each project group. Separating programmers and analysts allegedly provides more expertise in each area and more flexibility in assigning programmer resources. But this structure sacrifices singular accountability for the results of a project effort and leads to finger pointing. Coordination of a project is much more difficult, and separating programmers and analysts can lead to a self-assumed aristocracy on the part of the analysts.

The project control requirement must prevail, and whatever the arguments, the development section must be organized along project lines. How project groups are organized depends on the nature and the volume of projects. The number of analysts and programmers is a direct function of the estimated man-months of work to be completed.

If only a few users are served and the activity of each is sporadic, projects might be assigned at random. When larger numbers of users exist or when one or more users are highly active in terms of requirements, assigning project groups to support certain users is most effective. For example, a development section in a manufacturing company may have one project group to develop process control systems, one for financial applications, one for order entry/inventory, and so on. This organization allows the systems staff to begin to develop expertise in the application area and to develop better user relationships through repeated contacts. Figure 3-4 summarizes the organization of the systems development group discussed to this point.

There is an important distinction in function between the systems manager and the project manager. The systems manager plans application requirements, assigns resources to projects, and directs the overall activities of the project teams. The project manager

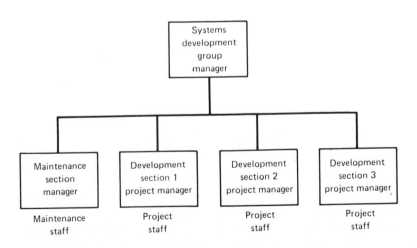

Figure 3-4. Systems development group—variation one.

normally is responsible for a single project effort. He plans the detailed execution of the project, specifies assignments to programmers and analysts, and performs detailed reviews of project outputs. In the smaller organization, one individual fulfills both functions. As the organization gets larger and the number of analysts and programmers increases, project managers must be added to the structure.

Ideally, the project manager should have one project active at a time. When project teams comprise less than five people, this may not be possible, as overhead becomes too great for the size of the project. One alternative is to use a project leader instead of a project manager to control the project, the distinction being that the project leader has the responsibilities of the project manager, but is also expected to perform analyst and programmer duties part of the time. Another approach to managing small project groups is to assign several small projects to a project manager. However, to maintain a reasonable span of control, the aggregate staff should not exceed approximately eight people, and there should be no more than three projects.

Sometimes a single project will be of such a magnitude that a large number of analysts and programmers are required. If the number of analysts and programmers exceeds ten, the team is too large to be supervised by the project manager. In that case another level of supervision may be required. Perhaps a lead programmer could be appointed to have primary responsibility for programming. There are countless variations depending on the situation and the skills of the individuals. The point is to maintain a reasonable span of control so as to achieve effective supervision.

The largest EDP departments have such a high level of project activity that more project managers are required than the systems development group manager can supervise. Then a management level is required between the systems development group manager and the project manager. The individual at this level is designated a systems development section manager. The number of individuals at this level is a function of the number of project managers, but by definition of their purpose, there would always be more than one. Project managers should be grouped under systems development

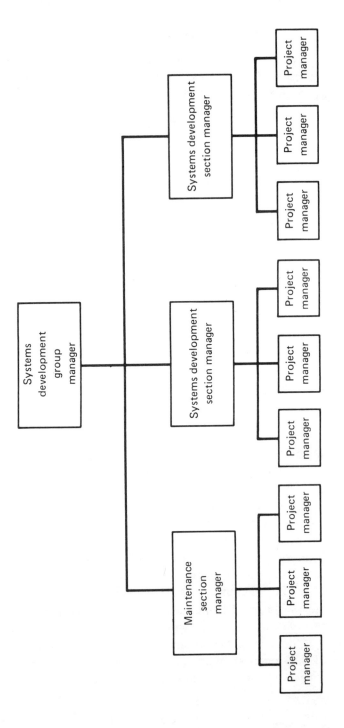

Figure 3-5. Systems development group—variation two.

section manager according to types of systems and users served. The systems development section manager then assumes the function of the systems development group manager for his application area. The systems development group manager's responsibilities then broaden to include the overall direction and coordination of development activities.

Similarly, at some point the maintenance section can reach the size requiring a second level of management. Project managers, also organized by application functions, fill this need.

Figure 3-5 illustrates the systems development organization in a very large EDP department.

ORGANIZATION OF THE COMPUTER SERVICES GROUP

The organization summary in Figure 3-2 lists six principle activities for the computer services group: receiving and key-converting input, maintaining data files, processing computer runs, dispatching output, maintaining hardware, and hardware analysis. Customer service was later added to this. Each of these activities requires certain knowledge and skills, and all resources, such as computer hardware, must be used optimally. For these reasons, computer services is never organized along application lines as the systems development group is. It is organized to create specialties in personnel. Individuals are assigned duties within computer services according to the activities for which it is responsible. Then applications are processed in a "job shop" mode, with one individual designated to schedule and oversee the flow of work. Personnel in the smaller shop report directly to the manager of computer services. Again, as the size grows, the organization structure becomes more complex.

The activities of computer services can logically be divided into three sections: data conversion, production control, and computer operations. Data conversion assumes the key-convert activity. Production control is responsible for customer service, receiving input, maintaining data files, and processing output, in addition to the

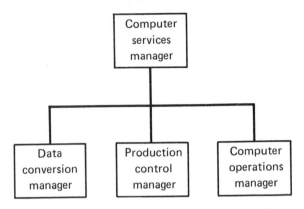

Figure 3-6. Computer services group—variation one.

important task of scheduling. Computer operations, as the computer processing arm of the group, maintains the hardware and is responsible for hardware analysis.

Figure 3-6 depicts the basic structure for the larger computer services group. As the size of the group continues to grow, in terms of volume, hardware, and personnel, subordinate supervisory levels may be required. These decisions are based on the number of people performing an activity and the requirements to limit span of control. In the case of the data conversion section, which performs a standard function, the manager can supervise 12 to 15 operators effectively. In production control, where numerous activities are performed, or in computer operations, spans of control will be smaller.

The Multishift Problem

To respond to user requirements of overnight turnaround and to utilize the hardware well, computer services often works multiple shifts and weekends. The multishift operations create a serious organizational question. How are the activities organized to ensure functional as well as operational coordination?

If the organization in Figure 3-6 is carried to a three-shift operation, each section manager appoints a shift supervisor to direct the section on each shift, and the section manager directs the overall function. This provides sound functional management but leads to many difficulties on night shifts, because there is no general coordination of operations. Typically, conflict and finger pointing ensue, problem solving suffers, and accountability is difficult to pinpoint.

The alternative is to have a supervisor on each shift for each section and have these supervisors report to a shift manager. This establishes one individual on each shift with full operational authority and accountability. The shift managers report to the manager of computer services; the section managers don't exist within this structure. There is an important weakness in this organization. The responsibility for functional coordination falls back to the manager of computer services. Who will provide the planning of schedules as guidelines to shift operations, set keypunch standards and hardware utilization standards, or develop procedures for tasks such as tape library control or scheduling?

Either alternative has serious drawbacks. Some organizations have tried a hybrid structure, superimposing shift management on the section management organization. This can only lead to chaos and internal conflict, because no one knows who reports to whom.

The predominant consideration is the need for a well-managed production environment. So, shift managers are most appropriate for the three-shift operation, although the functional-management problem cannot be ignored. Because the manager of computer services cannot possibly perform all coordination duties, another section must be established. This section is designated operations control and reports to the manager of computer services. Operations control prepares overall schedule plans and submits them to the manager of computer services for approval. It also provides support for developing operating procedures that affect only computer services, and implements them upon approval by the shift managers and the manager of computer services. Operations control can also provide administrative support such as tracking and reporting on on-order hardware.

The need for an operations control staff is a result of the peculiar requirements of the computer services organization structure. The section should not be allowed to attain undue autonomy within the EDP department and should never duplicate the activities of the EDP department staff support groups.

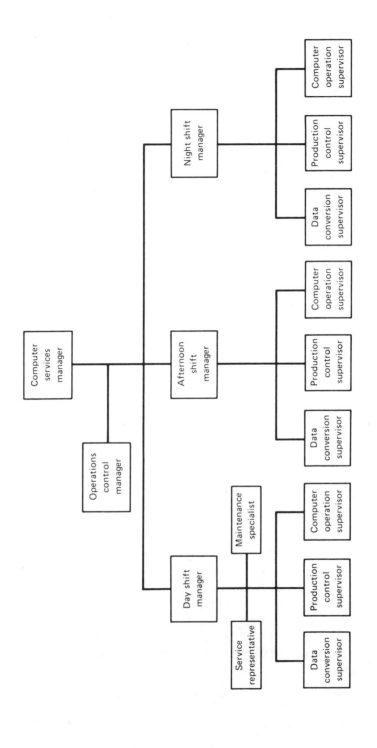

Figure 3-7. Computer services group—variation two.

Computer Services Specialists

Because of the highly complex nature of the large computer services group, the need for certain specialists may arise. The customer services representative has already been discussed. In an installation with considerable hardware changes, it may be advisable to add a hardware specialist to control the computer-room facility and installation projects. In very large installations, a hardware maintenance specialist can be invaluable to follow up and report on hardware downtime. Conversion specialists are vital in a group with a high conversion activity, and other specialists, permanent and temporary, can provide important support in computer services. These specialists can either be assigned to the operations control section or report to one of the shift managers. This depends on how much authority the manager of computer services wishes to delegate to the shift manager.

Figure 3-7 shows the organization structure for a very large computer services group and reflects the issues presented.

ORGANIZATION OF THE TECHNICAL SUPPORT GROUP

The organization of the technical support group is simpler than that of the preceding groups, principally because of the smaller number of people. The criteria for organization are technical. Smaller shops often feel that a systems programmer is an unaffordable luxury reserved for larger installations. This is true only in really small EDP departments. In any installation utilizing an intermediate or large computer, a competent systems programmer can easily be justified in terms of improved hardware utilization and technical problem solving. In smaller installations the technical support group may consist of only one systems programmer reporting to the director of data processing. As the installation grows and different technology is used, the technical support group becomes larger and more specialized.

Figure 3-8 suggests the proper organization for the technical support group.

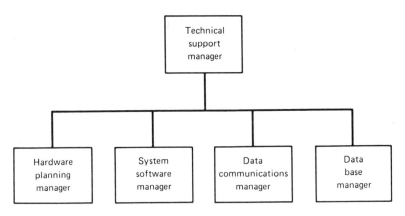

Figure 3-8.   Organization of the technical support group.

The hardware planning section is responsible for central and data-communication hardware. It analyzes new products, provides configurations to support processing needs, monitors utilization, and reports trends. This section must work very closely with all sections of data processing. The systems software section maintains operating system and general utility software. The data communications section maintains communications software and assists the systems development support group in the design of communications applications. The data base section maintains data base management software, plans data bases, and assists the systems development group in the design of data base application. To repeat, the inclusion of each section depends on the technology utilized in the department and, to some extent, on the computer vendor. Staff size within each section depends on the number of changes in hardware and control software and the number of applications to be developed.

EDP DEPARTMENT STAFF GROUPS

To complete our discussion of the organization of the EDP department, we need to take a closer look at the planning and administrative support groups. As discussed earlier, these are found only in large EDP departments. It is again important to emphasize the need to ensure that these groups are not misused in the department. Staff support groups misdirected or not directed at all can usurp the authority of the operating managers and result in severe internal conflict. The support groups should have specific responsibilities clearly differentiated from the operating groups. In effect, the support groups are an extension of the director of data processing, their function being to carry out some of the activities that would normally be his responsibilities. But they should never absorb any of his authority in respect to operating managers. A more detailed discussion of the activities of the staff support groups will clarify these important points.

The planning support group has two principal activities. It works with the director of data processing to develop long-range plans and budgets consistent with the business objectives. They also coordinate the preparation of annual or other periodic plans and budgets and consolidate these for the entire department. The planning support group understands the corporate objectives and the long-range strategic goals of EDP. It reviews planned programs of major users, with the cooperation of the appropriate systems development group, and determines potential EDP applications to support these plans. It conducts research on other companies' activities and provides recommendations for other effective uses of the EDP resource. It may perform a research study of a technology not yet used in the installation, such as data base management, and determine its feasibility, given the business objectives. The detailed technical evaluation of software should be left to the technical development group, however.

The planning support group might undertake a study to evaluate the place of new hardware concepts, such as distributed processing, in terms of how they relate to the growth of the company. However, detailed hardware evaluation and vendor selection would be left to the proper people at a later time. On the basis of executive decisions resulting from these studies, the planning group develops long-range programs and supporting budgets, with the participation of operating groups.

Specific short-term plans and budgets should be developed by operating managers. These plans are based on the long-range plans and other routine inputs. The planning support group assists in providing methodology for this activity and consolidating the plans of all groups into a departmental plan.

The administrative support group develops training and security procedures and, upon approval, administers them. It maintains contacts with agencies and other recruiting sources and provides candidates to fill open position. Hiring decisions are made by operating managers. The standards and procedures projects are undertaken at the request of the director or of group managers. These normally would be procedures affecting more than one EDP group. As discussed in respect to computer services, any group may develop its own procedures, but the administrative support group should be prepared to assist in requests of this nature to avoid a proliferation of staff positions within the department.

THE END PRODUCT

The definition of the internal structure of the EDP department is essentially complete. Figure 3-9 depicts the overall structure of a large EDP department. This illustration summarizes all the issues presented. The organization is designed to provide strong control, efficient communications, technical expertise, and responsive service at a minimum cost. As emphasized throughout, the structure will differ according to individual circumstances, but conducting an analysis along the lines in this chapter will yield an effective structure suited to the department's needs.

ORGANIZATION DOCUMENTATION

The final step in the development of the organization structure is the completion of organization documentation and procedures. These are detailed explanations of how the organization functions and interrelates. They are required to regulate relationships between users and EDP, among EDP groups, and within groups. Unlike operating procedures, which spell out the "how to," they are aimed at defining responsibilities and authorities, or "who will."

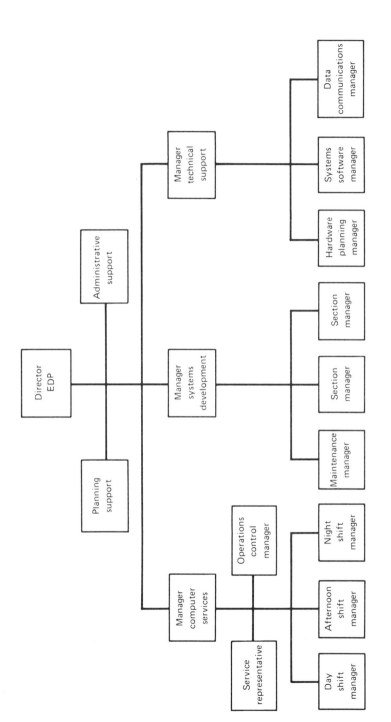

Figure 3-9. Organization structure of the EDP department.

Table 3-1 summarized the basic functions of the EDP organization. This level of detail is sufficient for the designer of the organization, but a much more detailed analysis is necessary for purposes of directing personnel. An easy way to complete this analysis is to prepare an organization/function matrix, with detailed functions listed vertically and the organizational entities horizontally. After an analysis of each activity, an "X" is placed in the column under the entity to which it is assigned. Once this detailed analysis is completed, job descriptions are prepared for every position in the department. Just as the organization/function matrix is used to assign department responsibilities to groups and sections, job descriptions allocate group or section responsibilities to specific individuals. Job descriptions also define those items that the individual is accountable for; therefore, they are also used in the important process of performance evaluation. This is discussed in a later chapter.

Even with these steps, more documentation may be needed to support the organization chart. The need to divide the hardware analysis function was presented earlier in this chapter. Table 3-2 showed specifically how these responsibilities are documented. An exhibit such as Table 3-2 should be prepared for any function where there may be an overlap of responsibility.

When all the documentation is completed, it should be assembled in an organization manual. The manual should be reviewed with all managers and be readily available to them. All the efforts advocated are for nothing if the structure is kept a secret after it is completed. Each employee should have a copy of his own job description and any other portion of the documentation relating to his own position.

USER RESPONSIBILITY

Up to now, when discussing the users of EDP, we have focused on the need to treat them as customers. But, as users, the other departments also have responsibilities for certain activities. Failure to define user responsibilities and to get users to meet those responsibilities causes many EDP projects to fail. Also, if the user role is not delineated and understood, EDP assumes the precarious role of being accountable for all problems.

In respect to systems development activities, the user is without question responsible for the definition of requirements and determination of whether system design output fulfills these requirements. A top-notch analyst will do his own investigation and make his own recommendations in respect to system facilities, but the ultimate responsibility is the user's, because only he knows what he needs.

In daily operations, the user should also have specified responsibilities. The computer services group must maintain certain run-to-run controls to ensure proper processing, but detailed reconciliation and data quality control must be with the user. Application systems should be designed with this in mind. Users must assume final responsibility for the accuracy of negotiable items and other reports sent outside the company, because the computer services staff cannot possibly be expert in every application system. Computer services should run every job routinely that can be scheduled according to predictable criteria. Users control job requests for those jobs whose frequency varies.

ORGANIZATION AND CHANGE

Now all aspects of the development of the EDP organization structure have been covered. One last issue must be considered. The environment of the EDP department is ever changing. Technology and work loads constantly change, often affecting the structure. Even the basic subdivision of functions into groups could change if the environment altered dramatically enough. Many factors are continuously testing the validity of the organization. The astute EDP director is constantly aware of this and includes a review of the organization structure as a routine portion of the planning process. Structural changes are planned and implemented as required, communicated to affected personnel, and reflected in the organization documentation.

-4-
EDP MANAGEMENT TECHNIQUES

EDP TECHNIQUES were previously defined as the procedures surrounding the use of computer resources. There are numerous techniques used in the EDP department, ranging from very detailed methods covering specific tasks to broad approaches affecting the entire organization. Some are documented in detail, and some are documented as general guidelines. The next three chapters deal with techniques of vital importance to EDP management. The intent of this book is not to attempt to define every procedure that might ever be used in an EDP department, but to discuss those fundamental to its effective operation. Other techniques, such as those concerned with control over negotiable instruments and with systems software maintenance, are provided by internal auditors and vendors, among others.

It would seem that a discussion of the need for formal methods in the EDP department is a waste of time, because the need is so obvious. However, there are many installations today that have very little or nothing in the way of formally documented practices. Personnel in these installations are given only broad direction and left to their own resources to perform duties. In other EDP departments, there might be procedures prescribing some of the most important activities, such as systems development and scheduling, but there is no systematic approach for controlling the overall activities and resources of the EDP department. The lack of formalization does not necessarily mean an absolute absence of technique, but the environment is highly dependent upon the experience and skills of individual employees.

Effective EDP management techniques are defined in this context as installation procedures, developed and documented, which are used to control the operation. They provide standardization of methods, training support, and, if carefully developed, the most effective methodology for the environment. The qualitative aspect is important because it is assumed that there is an optimum method for each activity. Chapters 4 through 6 deal with the important techniques required in an effective EDP department. Chapter 4 defines these techniques and analyzes those which are applicable to all EDP groups. Chapters 5 and 6 deal with techniques associated mostly with systems management and computer services management.

CONTROL PHILOSOPHY

Control in the broad sense is causing action according to a prescribed manner. The techniques to be discussed are aimed at providing the essential control over the key activities in an EDP organization. Prior to developing specific control procedures, a philosophy of control must be established as a guideline. The organization must define the level of service it wants to maintain, the degree of assurance of continuity of its operation, and the desired precision of cost control, but, on the other hand, also the amount of freedom it wants to give its personnel.

Some managers and users expect zero defects out of the EDP department. Without consciously defining a zero-defects policy, they act traumatized with every error discovered, even though some are inconsequential. User mentality, in certain cases, is, "If I don't scream, they won't give me the proper attention, and if I overlook anything, they will eventually get worse." On the other hand, daily operations are such a struggle in some EDP departments that EDP managers sometimes feel the user should be grateful he received reports at all, far less be concerned that they were a couple of hours late, that there weren't enough copies, or that the reports had been skillfully shuffled, requiring an all-day sorting operation.

Neither of these attitudes is appropriate, and neither is beneficial to the company as a whole. The EDP department must provide quality service to its users. In the short run, EDP may occasionally encounter difficulties that are disruptive to the user, but these situations must be quickly resolved. In the long run, the user should not be asked to accept excuses of circumstances "beyond EDP's control," because in the long run there is no such thing. The EDP department must manage its own operations effectively and control the performance of its vendors. On the other hand, the user, who is also a part of the same company, guided by the company's objectives, must be reasonable in his demands. Certain environments require a zero-defects operation, but this approach cannot be cost-justified in a commercial environment. The required redundancy of hardware and overhead of control personnel make zero defects simply prohibitive.

The ideal environment is one in which EDP and users agree upon reasonable service standards, measure performance against those standards on a regular basis, and judge performance on the basis of results. In this mode, it is agreed that individual problems will be reported and promptly resolved, but not used as an issue to put the EDP department on trial. As a part of establishing its control philosophy, each EDP department must quantify these standards. The optimum standards, subject to sound judgment, are the ones which provide reliable service at the least cost.

Due to the importance of the EDP department, controls must be established to ensure its continued operation to some reasonable extent. Disruptions to data processing installations can range from the absence of a key individual, to hardware malfunctions, to acts of God. Certainly, any installation would want to have the appropriate cross-training and documentation to ensure that the absence of any person is not unduly disruptive. But most installations probably cannot afford to fully provide for contingencies such as nuclear warfare. Each EDP organization must initially evaluate the importance of its existence to the company, the amount of time it can afford to be down, and the risks it faces. The evaluation of the probability and potential cost of each risk provides a basis for determining what type of procedures are necessary. There are many methods available for this risk analysis, and every EDP department should perform one. General policies regarding risk will affect many of the routine procedures of the data processing installation.

Cost control philosophy has an impact on procedural considerations too. No EDP department would ever allow anyone who desired hardware to purchase it, but it doesn't make sense, at the other extreme, to ration pencils to programmers. A proper procedural balance is to control the expenditure of major costs to prevent unwarranted significant expenses, and to provide guidelines for other expenditures and take corrective action as necessary on an exception basis. Management simply cannot review every expenditure prior to its occurrence.

The environment created as a result of controls is an important consideration of control philosophy. EDP personnel on the whole think of themselves as professionals, and in fact many of them are. It is easy to overreact and change an environment that is totally unstructured to one so wrought with procedures that there is no room for creative freedom. EDP professionals treated as juveniles will not perform to their potential. There are many ways in which personnel considerations conflict with goals related to maximizing service, controlling costs, and protecting operations. Personnel cannot be expected to completely sacrifice personal lives in the long run because of unreasonable demands of users under the guise of customer service. Purses of all personnel entering the computer room cannot be searched because of the possibility that one might conceal a bomb. And if time clocks are installed to ensure that everyone works nine to five, that is what everyone will do, including those who might otherwise have given extra effort.

The point of this is that a well-motivated staff allowed certain freedoms will contribute to customer service, protection against disruptions, and cost control. Well-motivated people are in some ways the most effective control. This is not a contradictory argument. Certain activities must have formalization and structure, but control for its own sake is counterproductive in the long run.

In summary, the appropriate control philosophy is one that provides a system maintaining a high level of customer service at a reasonable cost, ensures against disruption from probable risks, and controls costs while maintaining an environment where personnel can perform effectively. The techniques presented in this book are designed with this in mind. The use of these, as well as other, controls must be evaluated in relation to the installation's own philosophy. With a philosophy established, specific controls can be developed.

THE MANAGEMENT OF CHANGE

Of all the techniques of importance to EDP, management of change is probably the most vital. Dynamic EDP departments almost by definition are in a constant state of change. New applications, hardware configuration modifications, upgrading of systems software, and employee turnover are a way of life. From a general management viewpoint, change is the most difficult management challenge. Failure to manage major changes effectively is the nearly universal cause of operational disruptions, and certainly major change is the last straw for an organization already flirting with collapse. On the whole, the EDP industry and the business community generally don't do a good job of implementing change.

What does management do wrong to cause these failures, or at least to allow them to continue? First, management often does not get involved early enough to understand the project being undertaken and to head off problems before they occur. Second, management often imposes unreasonable deadlines, causing project members to take shortcuts and make careless errors. Third, budgets and schedules are frequently too strict to allow appropriate testing, verification, and implementation backup. But management's biggest failure is to continue to tolerate the catastrophies.

Rules of Management of Change

In order to ensure successful conversions, management must establish reasonable schedules, approve sufficient budgets, and get involved. Also, management must use sound techniques for managing change. There are several important principles, or musts, of change management, which we will discuss in this section.

The rate of change must be regulated. There are often several changes happening within a relatively short time within an EDP department. This is especially true in the large installation or the one undergoing a major overhaul. However, there is a limit to the amount of change that can be assimilated by any group, be it EDP or user, so the amount of change happening simultaneously must be regulated. The director of EDP must ensure that various sections of EDP are not working independently and planning simultaneous conversions affecting the same users. "Take one thing at a time" is a good guiding philosophy. If a user has just undergone a major personnel reorganization and the majority of employees are new to their positions, it is not an ideal time to implement a new computer application. A new operating system shouldn't be implemented during the conversion of a major new application system. If a new computer is being installed, it is well to delay installation of an on-line system that is required to be highly reliable.

Those in control of a major conversion must be experienced. Too often a conversion team rebuilds the wheel when a project has been previously undertaken by another company or even by someone within the company. The experiences are not reviewed thoroughly enough, if at all, so the same mistakes are repeated. Managers responsible for conversions should be well schooled in conversion techniques. Whenever possible, individuals who have completed similar conversions should be consulted for their experience. And when a highly technical conversion is undertaken, there is no substitute for having someone experienced in the relevant technology on the project team. For instance, if a totally different operating system is installed, training courses provided by the vendor teach the basics of the technology, but they just don't yield the in-depth understanding needed to avoid numerous pitfalls, so experienced support is required. Maybe the vendor can provide this support, but if not, a first-rate consultant or an addition to staff can bring a bag of tricks invaluable to the effort.

The departments, groups, or other units involved in the conversion must be stable. Too often a conversion is attempted when the EDP group or the user department is plagued with other problems or operating weaknesses. If a conversion is attempted in such a situation, its probability of success is substantially lessened, and the conversion itself is likely to topple the department completely. Some solutions, even if temporary, to existing operating problems must first be implemented before the conversion. When the instability is in the user department, a delicate situation can emerge for EDP. As a customer, the user may resent allegations by EDP that problems exist. Also, if the conversion is perceived as a solution to recognized problems, the user may balk at anything that delays implementation. Skillful diplomacy may be required to persuade user management to slow down. But a delay is necessary if the user is not ready. In the final analysis, EDP has a responsibility to the overall company goals and, as a last resort, should escalate the matter with a presentation to top management of its evaluation of problems and risks.

Budgets and schedules must be realistic. To some degree, schedules can be adjusted by varying resources, although there is a limit to how many people can effectively work on any project. Within guidelines established and subject to review, schedules and budgets should be developed by the project team. Project plans should include ample time and resources for adequate testing, documentation, training, and methodical conversions.

Conversion plans must be reviewed. No one person, or even any group, can ever expect to have the best ideas about everything. A conversion team can sometimes underestimate the complexity of the project because of inexperience, or it can become overly optimistic because of pressures caused by schedule slippages or budget over-runs. To avoid errors in judgment caused by these misperceptions, conversion plans must be reviewed by individuals who are skilled in conversion techniques and independent from the project. This requires a tactful approach to be effective. Reviewers must critique carefully and constructively. On the other side of the coin, those being reviewed must accept suggestions as an aid rather than as a challenge. For a conversion to be successful, *the plan must be communicated.* Every individual involved must know the overall approach, his specific responsibilities, and the timing required for his tasks. Each individual must communicate progress and problems to the project manager. Changes to the plans must be clearly and quickly communicated to everyone.

Expectations reflected in conversion plans must consider people.

People at all levels are affected by change to some degree. Social relationships are disrupted if work assignments change and anxiety arises when job content that was once mastered is changed. Training and explanations of the conversion certainly help, but people still will be somewhat unsettled in the process of change. This is not concerned with the learning curve but with the factors that inhibit learning. The emotional factor often explains why people don't grasp new procedures that should be simple to learn.

Plans must consider the learning curve. This follows logically from the preceding principle. Even when procedures are simplified, operations may slow down during the transition, while employees become comfortable with the new procedures.

Plans must consider the additional work load caused by the conversion. The departments involved in the change have ongoing responsibilities and generally are staffed accordingly. Assuming a currently efficient staff level, there is no reason to expect that the additional work load of the conversion can be handled by the current staff. Yet time and again conversions are attempted in this manner. The amount of extra work directly resulting from the conversion activity, emotional factors, and the slowing effect of the learning curve on operations must be considered and the staff levels temporarily adjusted accordingly. What's required is the same realistic attitude as in determining schedules and resources for the project team.

The conversion team must train users and others thoroughly to ensure a successful conversion. User department personnel, computer services employees, and the staff responsible for ongoing maintenance of the system must be trained by the development team. Documentation of the procedures is a training aid, but procedures are really more valuable as an ongoing reference aid *after* training. To their chagrin, many project teams have written weighty documentation, turned it over to users, and then watched them fumble through the initial implementation. They didn't realize that they didn't really train.

There are many training techniques that should be considered. Perhaps the most valuable is to get as many people involved in the development of the project as early as possible. There is no substitute for the insight gained from taking part in decisions regarding the design and purpose of a system. Prior to implementation, formal training sessions should be conducted for everyone. These sessions cannot be merely system overviews and include all personnel regardless of position. One or more sessions should be designed to train in detail each individual who will be affected by the new system. These sessions must cover the overall system and specific procedures for operations. Too often, project teams are overoptimistic and do not include procedures for what to do when something goes wrong. This is the failure of many training programs which teach only the processing steps under normal conditions. But surely, something will fail, so the project team must be imaginative about analyzing the system, anticipating error situations, and developing recovery steps, and all of this must be included in training programs and procedures.

Training programs must allow for repetition, because people cannot be expected to learn everything in one session. An old axiom of political speech writing is relevant here. It says, "Tell them what you are about to tell them, tell them, and then tell them what you just told them." After that, give them a chance to ask questions. Learning is doing, so personnel should be active in the test and parallel phases whenever possible. Specific training aids such as audiovisuals, training exercises, and the like should be carefully selected. At least for major projects, a training professional should be consulted.

Training does not end when implementation begins. Regardless of the quality of training, people will have a mountain of questions with the new system once it begins live operation, often to the bewilderment of the project team. Responding that the question was covered in training or is in the procedures manual may be emotionally satisfying, but it does not contribute to a successful conversion. The project team must be present during the implementation, patiently answer questions as needed, and show the staff how to use the documentation provided as questions arise.

To minimize risk, the project team must implement plans slowly. Whenever possible, the implementation should take one small part at a time. Phase hardware changes, convert a section at a time when implementing a new application system, and implement new systems software on one machine at a time in a multiple-CPU environment. The objective is to minimize the impact of problems and to isolate problems at a manageable level.

Finally, successful change management must provide backup. As a part of conversion planning, the procedures must include an analysis of what can go wrong and what the fallback approach is. This is vital to user service, because the EDP department cannot guarantee that there will be no problems, but it must ensure that these problems never bring disaster to users.

Figure 4-1 is a checklist of the musts of change management. Conversion plans, of course, include the details of who does what. The checklist provides a guideline of what must be done. In the EDP environment, these fundamental principles seem to be ignored to some degree in most situations. Therefore, the successful EDP department must establish a technique to ensure proper conversion approaches. Because all EDP groups initiate changes requiring top-level coordination, and because change management is so vital to the success of the EDP department, top EDP management must get involved in this activity.

The rate of change must be regulated.
The project team must be experienced.
The environment must be stable.
Budgets and schedules must be realistic.
The project team must be reviewed.
Plans must be communicated.
Plans must consider people.
Plans must consider the additional work load.
The project team must train all groups affected by the conversion.
The project team must implement plans slowly.
Plans must provide backup.

Figure 4-1. The musts of change management.

INSTALLATION MANAGEMENT COMMITTEE

In order to ensure that the participation of EDP management is regular and ongoing, a permanent installation management committee should be established within the EDP department. This committee should meet on a weekly basis. It should be chaired by the director of EDP and include all group managers. Other key managers and personnel may be included on a permanent or temporary basis. The director of EDP should appoint someone to provide staff support for the installation management committee. In a larger shop, the manager of planning support would perform the duties.

The first responsibility of the installation management committee is to regulate the rate of change. During the departmental planning cycle (discussed in Chapter 9), a schedule of all conversions should be prepared showing all implementation time frames. This schedule is reviewed at the time of planning to ensure that no group is subjected to too much activity at once. The installation management committee monitors project progress and adjusts schedules to account for changes in individual project time frames. An easy way to do this is to prepare a simple Gantt chart showing conversion schedules for all projects. Whenever there is more than one simultaneous conversion, the groups that will participate are identified. If any group is to be involved in more than one of these simultaneous conversions, close scrutiny and possible adjustments are required. The committee must review the scope of each conversion and the conversion plan of the project team. The committee must see to it that each item in Figure 4-1 is reflected in the conversion plan and must make qualitative evaluations. No conversion should proceed without this evaluation.

PROBLEM CONTROL

Closely related to change management are the techniques relating to problem management and problem control. No matter how competently managed, each EDP department has its share of problems, ranging from hardware failures to program bugs. Some of the problems require immediate attention, others have lower priority. Because problem control is so vital to the effective EDP organization, it also requires top EDP management attention. The previously defined installation management committee with its weekly meetings is a good vehicle for problem control.

With this additional responsibility, the committee may want to include a representative from the major hardware vendor, depending on the vendor relationship. The committee has two roles relating to problem control. First, it reviews all open problems and ensures that proper corrective steps are being taken. Second, it reviews trends of problem history and directs steps to resolve serious reoccurring problems as necessary. At each weekly meeting, the committee reviews open items as of that date. It also reviews statistical summaries of problem history. In a later chapter, procedures for documenting and reporting problems are presented.

Some might object to the delegation of important responsibilities like change management and problem control to a group designated as a committee. These people may be more comfortable referring to this as a weekly management meeting or something similar. Whatever the designation, the functions are the same. Furthermore, each manager is strictly responsible for his own area. The director of data processing solicits, and listens to, the opinions of others, but he maintains ultimate authority. There is no vote taking.

Problem-Solving Strategy

Problem-solving approaches require some consideration of strategy. Upon analyzing problem trends, EDP management must determine whether "quick fixes," long-term solutions, or a combination of both are the best approach. Quick fixes are short-term steps that are exceptions to the normal control process but taken to eliminate problems. For example, if a recently implemented accounting system is plagued by production delays as a result of various errors in computer services, some short-term action may be required. Perhaps a systems analyst or other senior person must be assigned to monitor all aspects of processing and ensure timeliness. Some problems are not fixable in the short term. If a technical development group is bogged down with vendor-supplied modifications to systems software, possibly only a long-term program will show any improvement. In a situation where an EDP department finds itself unable to supply programmer test time, a combination of both approaches is required. A quick fix would be the purchase of outside test time, and the long-term solution would necessitate an analysis of hardware capacity and appropriate scheduling or configuration changes.

The key is that problem resolution must be approached according to the circumstances. When a section is bogged down, simply telling personnel to improve quality or whatever probably will not bring about the entire result. The cause of problems must be identified. In some cases, especially when user service is involved, quick fixes must be defined. The user cannot be expected to suffer while EDP lays out long-range plans. However, other problems may not be important enough to disrupt activities, and their solution may be scheduled as an addition to the next version of the EDP plan.

SECURITY, BACKUP, AND RECOVERY

Another important area of EDP procedures is the security, backup, and recovery plan. As a part of every application design, file retention and backup procedures are developed. The EDP department must also establish backup and recovery techniques for threats to the continuity of its operations. If EDP management does not give attention to these areas, the auditors most certainly will someday. The subject of disaster management is most relevant for the computer services group, although some attention must be given to development groups. (Imagine the loss of man-hours if a fire occurred in the systems group at night, destroying all materials relating to a very large project just before the completion of coding!)

Earlier in this chapter, risk analysis techniques were mentioned. Without attempting to go into detail, it is worth noting the types of threats to EDP departments. EDP operations are potentially disrupted by anything that threatens any or all of the department's resources. These resources are personnel, hardware, programs, documentation, and the physical facility. Threats fall into categories of errors and malfunctions, accidental damage, sabotage, employee relations problems and work stoppages, acts of God, and acts of war or civil disorder. Every EDP department must perform its risk analysis, but there are certain measures that are basic to every installation.

EDP management must develop its security systems to limit risks. Every computer room should be built with fire protection as part of the design. Automatic fire detection and suppression systems are an absolute must. Access controls are required to limit unauthorized traffic in the computer room. Documentation must be carefully controlled and its use restricted. Employees must be cross-trained. Key data files must be controlled to prevent accidental destruction or unauthorized access. These steps are an absolute minimum to protect the data center.

No matter what security measures are taken, no installation is ever fail-safe. Therefore, backup techniques must be installed to allow recovery from a disruption. Operational backup should be considered in the configuration of the hardware. Additional hardware can minimize disruptions due to malfunction, but the cost of total redundancy is prohibitive for most companies. Mutual-assistance arrangements with other companies can be used for short-term and long-term requirements, although inherent in these arrangements is the risk of disruption because of problems in another company. A list of service bureaus and vendor data centers that can back up processing should be maintained.

EDP departments that are vital to their companies should consider construction of a partial or complete backup computer-room facility with air conditioning and power. Although this is expensive, the lead time to complete this construction could be disastrous if the computer room and the building were seriously damaged by a fire. An understanding should be reached with vendors on lead times and procedures for the replacement of equipment beyond repair.

All these steps are important; but the most vital backup system is the one for data, software, and documentation. In a disaster, a company can somehow beg, borrow, or buy time on computers and get supplies. But no one else can replace the data and programs for the company. Imagine a devastating fire that destroys the computer facility and files of major users. Can the company continue to conduct business? If all software had to be recreated, the expense would be enormous and the development time would be absurd considering the circumstances. A secure backup data library in a controlled physical environment should be maintained by every company that has a computer operation. In fact, any company needs a facility like this, even if it doesn't have a computer. The remote library should contain recent copies of all data files, programs, and documentation. The library should be updated as frequently as necessary to maintain it as a viable backup tool. In large companies with many daily processing applications, the remote library may require daily updating. There is a cost to this, but it is so vital, it is an absolute necessity.

Because the remote library is unimportant to daily operations, it may not get urgent attention on an ongoing basis from the computer services staff. Strict controls and constant management review will be required to ensure that it is properly maintained. Possibly an independent party, such as an internal security group, should be responsible for this activity.

Once backup facilities are in place, disaster recovery plans need to be documented. Since many different kinds of disruptions can occur, the plans cannot anticipate every situation. Disaster plans should be written as guidelines for developing more specific plans in a given situation. They should include a definition of responsibilities for disaster recovery and possibly a special organization structure. The names and phone numbers of backup facilities, vendors, and others required for recovery should be included. Also, a general guideline for priorities and procedures is needed. The plan obviously will require continuous updating. Recovery can be an extremely expensive operation. Insurance policies are available to cover many of these costs at a reasonable rate. It is worthwhile to investigate these options.

INSTALLATION DOCUMENTATION

Throughout the discussion of controls and control techniques, continuous reference has been made to the importance of documentation. Documentation of procedures is an important and necessary activity. But if this documentation is to be useful, it too must be controlled. The documentation must be up to date and accurate, understandable, and available. Standards for format and content of documentation are required.

Documentation should be maintained in a central library. In a small shop this may be a file cabinet; in the larger one it could be a room with special filing equipment. In either case, the master copies should be controlled by a designated person. Documentation should be signed out by the user for a specific period of time. If it is not returned, the librarian should follow up. This library should contain documentation on applications as well as on procedures, and copies of all material should of course be kept in the off-site library.

In order to ensure that documentation is maintained, controls must be in place to guarantee that the master documentation is changed every time procedural and application modifications are made. A convenient way of doing this is to have the librarian sign off on all changes to state that documentation changes have been received. These procedures will vary with type of change.

SELF-AUDIT

Thoughtfully designed procedural controls are mandatory in the effective EDP organization. But they must be *used* to have any value. Unfortunately, many people cannot be convinced that these procedures are not mostly a waste of time. Others understand the value but short-cut controls and allow them to become obsolete because of the pressures of day-to-day activities. There is also an ironic psychology that stresses the use of a given control procedure when problems exist, and suggests that they are not necessary when problems disappear. In the long run, people seem to lose perspective of the cause-and-effect relationship between the controls and satisfactory performance.

Assuming, then, that human nature tends to allow controls to slip over a period of time, they must be monitored. In other words, the controls must be controlled. One way of doing this is for management to actually walk around and see how things really happen as

THE EFFECTIVE EDP MANAGER

opposed to what the procedures say. There is no substitute for first-hand reviews. Internal auditors will also provide periodic reports on control problems. But these alone will probably not be frequent enough to ensure consistent adherence to established procedures.

Another approach is for the director of data processing to establish a periodic self-audit with respect to controls. Monthly reports are ideal. The self-audit is conducted by someone familiar with all control procedures in the EDP department. A checklist is made of all control procedures and organized by the section responsible for them. On a monthly basis, the forms, documentation, and use of each procedure are observed. The utilization of the procedure is then rated on a scale from 1 to 3. A rating of 1 means that the procedure is being carefully followed. A rating of 2 indicates that the control is used enough to maintain the intent but minor variations were observed. Ratings of 3 are for procedures not followed closely enough to maintain the intended control.

Reports from the self-audit are distributed to all group managers as well as the director of data processing. Group managers are obligated to prepare a memorandum to the director explaining all 2 and 3 ratings and propose plans for corrective action. If the director of data processing is firm in his support of this program, control should be measurably improved, and this means a more effective EDP department.

The techniques presented in this chapter are those which must be considered by every EDP organization. If properly applied, they will provide the foundation for a well-run shop.

-5-

Tools of Systems Management

IN ADDITION to the techniques discussed in Chapter 4, there are procedures relating more closely to the systems management function of the EDP department. In this context, systems management includes the systems development group and the technical development group, but systems management techniques are also applicable to some of the staff support functions of the larger EDP departments. Even though these groups deal with different technologies and perform different functions, their operations are of a similar nature, as are their control requirements. Computer services and the systems groups are distinctly different in nature. Computer services is the production arm of data processing, responsible for the "manufacturing" of the EDP products. The systems function is like "engineering," designing products and production tools. These two groups present different management problems and require different management techniques.

PROJECT MANAGEMENT

Systems functions have both development and maintenance responsibilities. In the development mode they are required to design and implement systems and technologies defined as projects in the EDP plan. If the systems function is to be successful, it must establish and fully utilize comprehensive project management techniques. There is no other procedure as vital to successful systems management as project management.

The objectives of project management are to ensure project completion according to schedule, adherence to budget, and assurance of the quality of end products. The two main elements of project management are planning of project activities and monitoring of project progress. To accomplish the objectives, project management procedures must do the following things:

- Define the activities and tasks to be performed and their sequence.
- Define the resources required for the completion of the project.
- Assign specific responsibilities for the completion of each task.
- Determine the schedule to be followed by the project.
- Provide for comprehensive reporting of project status at short intervals.
- Define interim end products to provide for short-interval quality reviews.

There are many different ways to design specific procedures to accomplish all these requirements, but no function can be excluded.

Before proceeding further with methodology, it is probably necessary to answer the objections of EDP people who would say that project management procedures are a waste of time and unnecessary paperwork. Some would contend that as professionals, they know how to do their jobs and will get them done as quickly as humanly possible. Arguments follow that there is no way to estimate EDP projects accurately because they are so complex. The answer to all of this is the same: Bunk!

The true professional understands the vital importance of project management techniques, and how sound use of the procedures will actually assist him in performing his job. The professional understands that without effective project management techniques he is likely to be under constant pressure from his own management and users because of schedule slippages and budget overruns. He knows the pitfalls of finding out late in the development that a task was not completed properly or at all. And the professional has seen project teams operate in confusion because responsibilities were not well defined. The professional also knows that when he is competent in project management techniques, the procedures take relatively little time. He realizes that despite his experience, there is no substitute for a well-planned approach to project development, and that estimating can be reasonably accurate if done thoughtfully.

Project management techniques work for many reasons. The project planning phase provides an orderly sequence of tasks to be performed. The short-interval status reporting pinpoints problems early so that corrective action can be taken. Accountability is established for individuals as well as the project team as a whole. Project management techniques yield several other benefits. Good project planning provides the basis for allocation of resources for the group and is the foundation of the systems plan. Accurate project planning allows project activities to be coordinated with the users and to be considered by change management procedures. So, in addition to the obvious arguments for meeting deadlines, there are other considerations. Also, systems management must realize that people simply perform better when they have specific objectives. When project management techniques are used, team members are paced throughout the project, not only during the last-minute rush when the final deadline approaches. Finally, project management techniques establish a basis for quantitative performance measurement.

The justification here is intentionally lengthy, because there is still an amazing amount of apathy and resistance to sound project management in the EDP community. For those who were previously or are now believers, the next discussion centers around project management procedures. Those not yet convinced may as well skip to the next topic.

As noted earlier, there are many specific methodologies for project management that are effective. PERT/CPM techniques are very effective and highly complex, but not necessary for anything other than the largest of projects. Larger EDP departments acquire automated project control systems, and there are several software pack-

PROJECT NAME _ _ _ _

PROJECT MANAGER _____

PHASE _____

BUDGET ALLOCATION _____

PAGE ___ / ___ OF

DATE ___ / ___ / ___

NO.	ACTIVITY/TASK DESCRIPTION	DEPENDS ON	ASSIGNED	MAN-	PLAN DATES					COMMENTS
					START	ACTUAL	COMPLETE	ACTUAL		

SUBTOTAL _____   GRAND TOTAL _____

Figure 5-1.   EDP project plan form.

ages on the market. These are useful from the standpoint of reducing clerical effort, but the same benefits can be obtained with a manual system.

A description of a relatively simple manual project control technique follows. This system has been used in an environment where major development activity was undertaken, and it was proved successful. This topic of project management procedures is so important that EDP departments must give priority to their implementation. If no one in the department is experienced in project management techniques, an experienced, reputable consultant to manage the implementation is a good investment.

Preparing Project Plans

An EDP project plan form is shown in Figure 5-1. This plan is completed at the onset of the project before any other project activity takes place. The project manager completes the plan, but as many of the members of the project team as possible should participate. This participation not only provides additional input but also ensures the team's commitment to the plan. The final plan should be reviewed and approved by the appropriate systems managers. Differences in opinions on approach and estimates should be thoroughly discussed and resolved at the outset.

The heads in Figure 5-1 are mostly self-explanatory, but two notes are appropriate. The "Phase" space is used when a very large project is divided into several smaller subprojects for planning purposes. Initially, a plan is laid out for the phases. Then a more detailed plan is prepared as each phase is undertaken. Progress of each phase is monitored in relation to the overall plan, and adjustments are made accordingly. A sample of this approach will be discussed later. The "Budget Allocation" space represents the estimate, if any, provided in the EDP plan. This information is only for comparative purposes to determine how the project plan relates to the overall plan. But the initial estimate is based on limited information and should not be construed as a final budget. The actual budget for project management purposes is the sum of approved task estimates as shown on the bottom of the form.

The "No." column is for the number of activities and tasks

69

defined for the project. The tasks are the actual steps to be followed to complete the project. Activities are merely groups of related tasks. The activity descriptions are optional and useful only to group and identify related tasks. Activity numbers are designated with alpha characters or Roman numerals. Tasks are numbered sequentially. Numbers increment for each task in the project plan, even if activities are shown. If this is not done, status reporting is cumbersome.

The "Activity/Task" column is for a description of steps to be followed for project execution. As mentioned, activity designations are optional. Task descriptions should clearly describe the action to be taken. Each task should also provide a tangible end product. This end product need not be a formal document, but each task should at least produce a worksheet displaying the results. Meeting this requirement takes some thought, but task descriptions such as "review this" or "talk to so and so" are next to useless for project management purposes.

The "Depends On" column is useful to the project team to ensure the proper order of tasks. The numbers of any tasks that must be completed prior to the given task are indicated here. If the numbers are greater than that of the given task, then there is a logic problem in the order of tasks. "Assigned" is for the name of the individual with primary responsibility for the completion of the task. This is important for tasks where more than one person will participate.

The "Man _____" column is used for estimates for each task. The dash is used to complete the description of the unit of measurement of estimates, such as Man-Month or Man-Day. The unit is chosen according to the size of the schedule, but man-days is probably the most appropriate for typical EDP projects. The initials of each person participating in the task and the estimated time for each follow. Tasks must be limited to provide short-interval reviews. A good guideline is to allow no task to exceed five man-days. If a task exceeds this guideline, it should be divided.

The "Plan Date" columns are extremely critical. They provide the start and stop dates scheduled for each task, as well as a place to record actual dates as the project progresses. The dates must be considered in relation to the estimates. Date scheduling is a function of two variables: the estimated work load and the amount of resource. As discussed with respect to the management of change, there are practical limitations, but dates can be varied as resources change. Therefore, the project manager must determine the parameters within which he is operating. If the date of project completion has been set, he must, on the basis of the total estimate, calculate the total number of people required to complete the project by this date and assign them to tasks to complete the project in the desired time frames. On the other hand, if personnel and other resources are restricted, then they are assigned to tasks sequentially and the date of completion results. A project plan developed on the basis of fixed resources and a firm schedule determined prior to estimating will inevitably lead to an unrealistic expectation.

There is unfortunately no precise formula for determining these dates. It is something of an art and requires experience. There are practical considerations such as the skills of individual team members, be they EDP or user personnel. For complex projects, a chart with dates and project team members on the axes is useful. As assignments are made, a line is drawn next to the name under the appropriate dates to indicate this assignment. In this way the project manager is sure that each resource is fully scheduled but not overloaded. When the project plan is completed, a Gantt chart reflecting the schedule of all tasks is a helpful review and double-check, as well as beneficial later in reviewing project progress. The project manager should review the Gantt chart in respect to the "Depends On" column of the project plan to ensure that no dependent task is scheduled before a required task.

For clarity, Figure 5-2 is provided as an example of a project plan. This figure, though simplified, shows the basic layout.

Project Estimating

It should be evident that the quality of estimating is a key to successful project management. The question is not whether the estimating can be done accurately, but at what point in the cycle of development it should be done. This is significant not only to management decisions and planning requirements, but also in the determination of the point at which the project team is accountable. The earlier an accurate estimate can be developed, the better.

There are questions of feasibility that management must make

71

Customer Statistics Report — PROJECT NAME

Joe Jones — PROJECT MANAGER

NO.	PHASE — ACTIVITY/TASK DESCRIPTION	DEPENDS ON	BUDGET ALLOCATION		PLAN DATES				COMMENTS
			ASSIGNED	MAN- J.J.	START	ACTUAL	COMPLETE	ACTUAL	
	I. DETERMINE REQUIREMENTS								
1	Document user data needs		J. Jones	1.0	1/15		1/15		
2	Document calculations		"	1.0	1/16		1/16		
3	Describe report	1,2	"	.5	1/17		1/17		
4	User sign-off	3	"	.5	1/17		1/17		
	II. DESIGN								
5	Detail report layout	4	"	.5	1/18		1/18		
6	Describe input files	5	"	.5	1/18		1/18		
7	Flowchart program	6	"	1.5	1/19		1/22		
	III. PROGRAM								
8	Code program	7	"	2.0	1/23		1/24		
9	Test and debug	8	"	3.0	1/25		1/29		
10	Document program	9	"	.5	1/30		1/30		
	IV. IMPLEMENTATION								
11	User documentation	10	"	.5	1/31		1/30		
12	Sign-offs and turnover	11	"	.5	1/31		1/31		
			SUBTOTAL	12.5	GRAND TOTAL	12.5			

Figure 5-2. Sample project plan.

judgments on. The earlier accurate estimates are made, the less chance of spending money on a system that is not cost-justifiable. Accurate early estimates are important to overall planning in both the EDP department and user departments. Firm early estimates are essential for proper accountability. Too early an estimate is unfair to the project team, and if the estimate is too late, it is virtually meaningless for this purpose.

Some EDP people would claim that firm estimates are not possible until after the system is designed. Others contend that the development must proceed as far as program design for an application system, because the programming phase is the most significant and programming cannot be estimated until detailed specifications are complete. Waiting until such a late point has serious disadvantages. A considerable amount has been spent before the feasibility of a project is determined. On large projects, this can be substantial. If it is determined that the project is not feasible, management must either scrap the project with nothing to show or risk going ahead with an unjustifiable system. (A common pitfall here is the "benefits to costs-to-complete" type of analysis used to justify continuation.) Also, EDP planning is difficult when personnel schedules cannot be planned in advance. Credibility is lost by shifting dates during project development. Sometimes equipment orders need long lead times, and later estimates may not be sufficient. In sum, it is highly desirable to make accurate estimates as early as possible.

Several factors contribute to the ability to make early estimates that are reliable. The more knowledge and experience the project team has relating to the process, the more accurate it can be. An application team with an extensive design and programming background can make better estimates. Familiarity with the requirements of the project is another asset. If a project manager has developed an accounts receivable system before, it is easier for him to estimate another accounts receivable project, even if it is different to some degree. Experience in the specific technology is also important. If a new language is used or an unfamiliar data base management system is anticipated, estimates cannot be as accurate. Knowing the capabilities of the project team members is important, so it is helpful if the project manager had prior experience with the team members.

What does a director of data processing or a systems manager do to promote reliable estimates early in project development? First, he ensures that the project team includes at least some highly experienced employees. On key projects, he relies on people proven in the department. He doesn't make a new hire the key man on a major project, if it can be avoided at all. If some people in the organization are familiar with the application area, they should be part of the team, provided they are available. Project team members should have completed all major technical training before the start of the project. This may sound unrealistic, but major technical approaches normally are defined by the type of project.

Organizing project teams as described here will contribute to giving the project manager some experience with team members before the project itself is started. Assuming that the conditions outlined are met, reasonable estimates can be made relatively early in the process. If none of them is met, the whole effort is shaky at best anyway.

The first steps in any project development are a systems planning phase and a requirements study. For small projects, these activities are the initial ones of the project plan; for large projects, they are included in separate project plans designed for the phase. In the systems planning phase, the project team defines the user's problem, reviews current operations, determines alternatives, and develops a reasonably detailed proposal. As part of this effort, the project team interviews users and others, within and outside the company, who may have pertinent expertise. In the requirements study, the team defines all user needs, including inputs and outputs. At the end of this effort, the team should have a good feel for the scope of the activity and should be able to prepare estimates. Assuming the previously discussed conditions are met, these estimates should be considered final.

The specific content of both the concepts and requirements studies need to be carefully considered. It is not necessary to design reports by this stage, but the team must know of each one required. If terminals are used, the number and type must be known. These studies must be very thorough. They are not quick reviews. The time spent up front is well worth the investment to provide a sound plan early.

All this needs a little perspective. Although the major systems will require this type of study, it certainly is not necessary for the smallest projects. A project to produce a simple report should be estimated with reasonable accuracy without much study. Plus, the cost of systems planning studies is really part of EDP research and development, so although some judgment in screening potential projects is required, don't get caught in the trap of doing feasibility studies to determine whether to do a systems planning study. And finally, don't set expectations too high. There is no way that all projects will be completed on schedule to the day and on budget to the dollar, no matter what is done. A reasonable guideline is that a project completed within plus or minus 10 percent of the plan is quite successful. It certainly is a dramatic improvement over some EDP departments' experiences. It is recommended that the high range be used for the plan and the feasibility decision, as it is always easier to accommodate an early finish or lower costs. In practice, project plans should be initially based on the real estimates, then the 10 percent should be added in some way as a contingency. In measuring the project team's performance, the plan including the contingency is used. With this adjustment, the team should be expected to complete the project within the limits of the plan.

Project Status Reporting

Once the project plan is completed, project management requires a method of reporting status. Quality, budget, and schedules are the elements requiring measurement. The project manager must ensure that all tasks have measurable end products. He also must be sure to review these task end products for completeness and quality. A group review of end products, with project team members and even others participating, is often useful at significant milestones of major projects. Schedule reviews are simply a matter of comparing the numbers of scheduled tasks with the numbers of those actually completed as of a given date. Short-interval budget review techniques require a little more thought.

Some project control systems compare the project budget with the expense to date. This approach is meaningless without some notion of how much of the work is complete. If a budget comparison shows half the budget spent, this tells nothing unless it is known whether half the work is complete, all of it, or none of it. Some systems break project budgets into weekly or other intervals and compare these with expenditures for the same period. This is merely a harder way to get the same meaningless result. It does not tell where the project can expect to be in respect to budget at its conclusion.

Some successful project control systems combine the budget-to-actual comparison with estimates of completion percentage. The project manager defines what percent of the work must yet be done and applies this to the budget. The figure predicted plus the actual spent should equal the budget. If it doesn't, the project is either over or under budget. But this technique takes a considerable amount of time to tally all outstanding tasks every reporting period.

There is a relatively simple technique that requires little calculation and quickly reflects budget status of the project. This technique uses an "earned hours" concept. The earned-hours percentage is a ratio of estimated tasks hours completed to paid hours. Keeping in mind that the project estimate is the budget, the ratio tells how much was spent to accomplish tasks in relation to how much was budgeted. In effect, the estimate is the standard of performance. For example, if a project team completed tasks aggregating 150 hours and 200 hours were paid for the period, the earned-hours measure is 75 percent. This does not say whether the project is on schedule or not, but it does indicate that the project is falling behind budget, because it is taking more manpower to complete tasks than was originally estimated.

A format for an EDP project status form is shown in Figure 5-3. Headings are simple. The first three columns are descriptive data relating to the project. One line is used for each project, as the form is intended to accommodate managers with multiple projects. Under "Task Status," the numbers of the tasks scheduled to date for the project are compared with those completed. The "to date" aspect is important so that overall status of the project can be evaluated. The tasks considered should not be just those for the current reporting period.

"Paid Hours" are the total paid hours of the project team for the period. Absences are included if paid, as well as overtime. Even time on other activities is included in paid hours if the team was

NO.	PROJECT	PHASE	TASK STATUS		PAID HOURS	HOURS ON PROJECT	HOURS EARNED	% TO PAID (1)	% EARNED (2)	% EARNED TO DATE (3)	COMMENTS
			SCHEDULED	COMPLETE							
TOTALS											

MANAGER _____

WEEK ENDING ___ / ___ / ___

(1) HOURS ON PROJECT DIVIDED BY PAID HOURS
(2) HOURS EARNED DIVIDED BY PAID HOURS
(3) TO DATE HOURS EARNED DIVIDED BY TO DATE PAID HOURS

Figure 5-3.   EDP project status form.

expected to work full-time. This is to highlight variances to schedules resulting from disruptions of unplanned and unbudgeted activities, and to control the occasional unscrupulous individual who would attempt to cloak a low percentage by alleging these conditions. This may distort total project costs a little, but it is the only way to ensure that scheduled resources are not dribbled away on unaccounted activities. "Hours on Project" are the number of hours estimated on the plan for tasks completed. No credit is given for tasks partially completed. The calculations for the last three columns are footnoted on the bottom of the form. The last column will require the project manager to keep a worksheet with aggregate totals of earned hours and paid hours. The paid-hours total is also useful to determine budget to date, when necessary.

The status report should be prepared on a regular weekly basis. The primary user of the status report is the project manager as its purpose is to summarize the status of the project and reflect areas where corrective action may be required to bring the project back on schedule. Further distribution depends upon the character of the department, but at a minimum the section or group manager to whom the project manager reports should receive a weekly copy. The director of data processing, if not on the weekly distribution list, should receive at least a montly report for all projects.

Analyzing Status Reports

The EDP project status report should be reviewed carefully every week by the managers who receive it. The short-interval scheduling and reporting concept is designed to allow early corrective action when a project is slipping. Overlooking the report, or simply noting problem areas and deciding to wait and see if they correct themselves, defeats the whole purpose. When schedule slippages or budget overruns become apparent, the project manager must determine what caused the problem and what alternatives for correction are available, and plan his actions. Higher-level managers should question the project manager and should not accept a "trust me, we'll catch up later" response. It is never too early in the project to correct a lagging effort. In fact, projects that start off behind schedule probably will never catch up if adjustments are not made early.

Managers who review project status reports are concerned with schedules and budgets. The "Task Status" column quickly reflects the schedule position, and the "% Earned" shows how the project is proceeding in respect to the budget plan. It is important to note that these are two independent measurements. A status report can show a project on schedule but behind in budget progress, or vice versa.

A "% Earned" figure of 100 percent means that the project is on plan in respect to budget. In other words, one hour of scheduled tasks is being completed for every paid hour. A percent figure lower than 100 percent means the project is over budget, and a percentage higher than 100 percent means the project is under budget. There are three reasons a project can vary from budget. First, if paid hours are used for activities other than the project, a variance will occur. A low "% Earned" figure caused by this situation will be reflected by a correspondingly low "% to Paid." Second, variances can be caused by problems in execution of the project. Third, the plan itself might be unrealistic. Assuming nobody is a superman or something on the other end of the spectrum, when percentages vary substantially from 100 percent, the plan is probably at fault. In any case, the situation must be analyzed and appropriate action determined.

The status report does not deal with dollars; it is an indicator of manpower budgets only. Therefore, a budget summary must be prepared periodically reflecting dollar costs for all project expense categories. Budget control will be discussed in more detail later.

Role of the Project Manager

There is one last element of effective project management that needs emphasis, and that is the importance of the project manager. Without an imaginative, aggressive project manager who effectively directs the work, closely coordinates activities, and responds to problems in an innovative manner, all methodology is virtually useless. Don't be trapped into believing procedures can substitute for this type of leadership. A top-notch project manager is the key to a successful project. His monitoring, prodding, and expeditious problem solving will head off slippages. His imagination will come up with effective responses to slippages that occur. The project manager must have a "will do" attitude, not one of "I'll try." His perception of problems and judgments regarding them really will make a difference, because there can be no formula to dictate the response for every situation.

A PHASED APPROACH
TO PROJECT DEVELOPMENT

Many EDP departments have adopted the so-called "phased approach" to project development. Nearly all real professionals in EDP advocate this method. Essentially, the phased approach provides a systematic development of a project, emphasizing substantial documentation of what is to be done before actually doing it, and providing planned review points. This method reduces risk of rework, or an end product unsatisfactory to its users, and provides the opportunity for a gradual commitment to the project development. The following list outlines the elements of the phased approach.

Systems Planning
    Define scope of project.
    Outline current operation.
    Determine problems and opportunities.
    Develop alternative solutions.
    Select approach from among alternatives.
    Identify costs and benefits.
    Recommendation.

Requirements Phase
    Detailed documentation of user's needs.
    Definition of inputs, outputs, and processes.
    Cost/benefits analysis.

General Design Phase
    Overall design of system.
    Detailed definition of products produced.
    Review cost/benefits analysis.

Detail Design Phase
    Detailed specification of system operation.
    (Program specs for programming project.)

Development Phase
    Completion of system.
    (Programming phase of programming project.)

System Test Phase
    Testing system in "live" environment.

Implementation Phase
    Installation of system.

Post-Implementation Phase
    Review of system in operation.
    Corrective action for operating problems.

Unlike the methods used in the data processing projects of earlier years, this method stresses the evaluation of the justification of the project and the precise definition of what is to be done before starting any work. Many people in the EDP field still argue against this approach, claiming that it simply is a waste of time. They say that they can start right with development after preliminary user reviews. This simply is not true. Logically, if the investigation and design phases are not thorough, chances for error and rework are much higher. Also, precise task definitions really always have to be made, no matter how the project is completed. People who say that the method is not necessary in reality are doing the tasks that should be completed during the earlier phases as they proceed with development—only they are much more prone to error without the more methodical approach. The phased approach is actually more efficient and will produce a higher-quality end product.

The preceding list shows that a cost/benefits analysis is performed during each of the first three phases. As previously stated, the project team is accountable for the estimates after the requirements phase. But the additional update is valuable as extra insurance, because it provides a point to abort the project if something unexpected appears. This is the "gradual commitment" aspect of the phased approach. Each phase should produce a tangible end product. The final product is complete documentation of each task in the phase.

This type of procedure is usually associated with the application-development activities of the systems development group. However, it is just as applicable to systems software and hardware configuration projects of the technical development group as well as various other projects in the EDP department. Systems programmers seem to be most resistant to this type of structure, but technical projects on the whole will also be more successful with the organized approach. Because of the differences in content, specific methodologies for the phases will differ by project type, but the general concept remains the same for all projects.

Although this book will not present specific methodologies for phased development, it is vital to understand the concept. A detailed methodology establishes the most effective and efficient techniques. It also standardizes the end products, which eventually become the system documentation, and therefore achieves standard systems documentation. A detailed methodology also provides a checklist of tasks for preparing the project plan. Methodologies for application development are commercially available from several places. Methodologies for other types of projects will probably have to be developed internally according to the needs of the particular department.

There is one additional benefit to the phased approach. It allows for easy subdividing of a project. When using this methodology, a project plan is prepared listing each phase, the planned start and stop dates, and the manpower of each phase. Then a plan is prepared at the beginning of each phase. The progress of each plan is reviewed against the objectives of the overall project plan.

EDP REQUEST PROCEDURES

The procedure for processing user requests is another important aspect of systems management. It has already been stated that the customer representative should handle production requests and problem reports. Now some technique is required to control requests for development activity. A request form is useful for this purpose, because it is a convenient means of controlling the processing of the request and provides a document of its finding, with approvals, for department records. Figure 5-4 is an example of a request form. This sheet can be used for users to request application development and for EDP departments to request technical development projects. All development work should be initiated with this request procedure. Minor maintenance projects can be requested via interoffice memo or by similar procedure, but systems managers must ensure that true development projects do not sneak in the back door in that manner.

The request for EDP systems form defines the procedure for processing requests. The requestor fills out the front side of the sheet, describing the request, the benefits, and the desired completion. The request is signed by an authorized member of the user department. It is advantageous to have one person in each user area approve all EDP requests; this avoids duplicate requests, assures EDP that the request is properly approved, and allows user management to protect against unwanted changes. The request is processed differently by the EDP department depending on whether it is a request for a new system, or a modification of an existing one. Both processes begin with the assignment of the investigation to a specific individual and the designation of a completion date for the response. This information is noted at the top of the second page of the form.

When processing a request for a new application, substantial investigation is required; therefore, the EDP department responds to these types of requests only in terms of whether an EDP systems planning study is warranted. If EDP does not feel such a study is warranted, "Not Recommended for Systems Planning Study" is checked. The reason for the recommendation is presented in the "Explanation of Findings" section, and the form is signed and sent to the user. If EDP concurs that a study is warranted, it so indicates by checking the "Recommended" box. An estimated cost for the study and its completion date are noted. Also, a broad range of costs for the entire project is presented. Although EDP cannot be at all accountable for this forecast, it can be useful to the user in that it puts the scope of the request in perspective. Any required comments are noted in the "Explanation of Findings" section before signing and sending to the user.

When analyzing a request for modifications to existing systems, a different approach is used. The assigned analyst reviews the request, defines the approach, and completes the cost estimate. Then the request is either noted as recommended or not recommended.

REQUEST TYPE

☐ New Application
☐ Modification to Existing Application — Identify _____

REQUESTING DEPARTMENT	DATE

DESCRIBE REQUEST

_____
_____
_____
_____
_____
_____
_____
_____
_____
_____

SAVINGS

Amount $_____

Period _____

Describe

_____
_____
_____

OTHER INTANGIBLE BENEFITS

_____
_____
_____
_____
_____
_____
_____
_____
_____
_____
_____
_____

REQUESTED COMPLETION DATE	SCHEDULED COMPLETION DATE (EDP ONLY)
REQUESTED BY	DEPARTMENT HEAD

Figure 5-4*(a)*.   Front of an EDP request form:
Request for EDP systems.

84

TOOLS OF SYSTEMS MANAGEMENT

DATE RECEIVED	ASSIGNED TO	DUE DATE

☐ New Application

System Planning Study — ☐ Recommended ☐ Not Recommended

Cost of Study — $ _____ Completion Date — _____

Preliminary Project Cost Range — From $ _____ To $ _____

☐ Modification to Existing Application

Cost Estimate

EDP Personnel	$	_____
User Personnel	$	_____
Computer Time	$	_____
Materials	$	_____
TOTAL	$	_____
Annual Operating Costs	$	_____

Completion of Request — ☐ Recommended ☐ Not Recommended

Explanation of Findings

_____
_____
_____
_____
_____
_____
_____

EDP PROJECT LEADER	DIRECTOR OF EDP	DEPARTMENT HEAD	USER
			☐ Does Concur ☐ Does Not Concur

Executive Action

_____
_____
_____
_____
_____
_____

Recommendation ☐ Approved ☐ Not Approved	By	Date

Figure 5-4(b). Back of an EDP request form:
Analysis of EDP request.

The "Explanation of Findings" section is used to define the approach to be used and the completion date for requests recommended, and to justify requests not recommmended in terms of cost/benefits or other consideration. In either case, when completed, the form is signed and sent to the user.

The user receives and reviews the completed analysis of the EDP request. If he concurs with the EDP finding, he so indicates and signs the form. The user may not concur with the EDP finding, in which case he notes this before signing. When the user does not concur with EDP findings, a meeting of the proper people should be held to try to resolve the difference. If resolution is not possible, an additional step is required. The limited veto power of the EDP department is somewhat inconsistent with customer service objectives, but is required because of the EDP department's responsibility to effectively utilize its resources. EDP must make every effort to keep this issue on the level of business discussions and in no way allow it to cause breaches in the user relationship.

Each company should establish a dollar amount under which a project can be authorized by the concurrence of the director of EDP and the user. When costs exceed this level, or when EDP and the user department cannot reach agreement, the request is forwarded to the appropriate executive officer (or committee if one exists). The executive officer reviews the request, the analysis, and the positions of the involved parties and makes the final judgment. He notes his decision in the "Executive Action" section, checks the disposition of the recommendation, and signs the form. At this point the request is dropped or worked into the EDP schedule according to planning procedures, depending on whether or not it was approved.

This discussion of the EDP request procedure has been on a rather general level. In actuality, a multipart form is required to satisfy all filing requirements and to control the process. A "tickler" file scheme is very helpful to track requests as they are processed. Detailed procedures should be prepared for this activity.

This concludes the discussion of systems management techniques. Along with due consideration of the EDP management techniques in the previous chapter, they provide the essential tools for an effective systems organizations.

-6-

Tools of Computer Services Management

As the production arm of EDP, computer services must develop techniques to plan capacity and control the production process. Because of its importance, hardware planning is covered in Chapter 8 under the broader subject of managing hardware resources. This chapter will begin with a presentation of computer services production control techniques and conclude with a discussion of issues regarding resources for computer services.

SCHEDULING

The organization of the computer services group, as defined in Chapter 3, was essentially along functional lines within shifts. This creates a production line environment, with specialties evolving for each processing step. But the job-shop type of approach requires coordination of workflow. This is carried out by the production control section, which is responsible for scheduling within computer services. The scheduling method adopted by this section is fundamental to its successful operation.

The first step in developing a scheduling methodology is to define the responsibilities and authorities associated with scheduling decisions. In the organization defined in Figure 3-6, the production control section is responsible for overall schedule planning. The more complex organization in Figure 3-7, designed for the larger multishift operation, has a more complicated distribution of responsibilities. Because schedule planning crosses shift lines, it is necessary to have one person responsible for the overall activity. A schedule analyst in the operations control section has this responsibility. The production control section of each shift is responsible for executing the jobs on its shift according to the plan and making any necessary judgments. All personnel are responsible for completing production according to schedules.

Before discussing a specific procedure, issues relevant to scheduling methodology must be considered. The earlier years of data processing were characterized by relatively small shops in comparison to today. Fewer jobs were processed, and the hardware resources were comparatively small and not nearly as flexible. Computers were limited in the number of jobs that could be run simultaneously, processing region sizes were often fixed, and peripheral-device assignments had to be individually controlled in many circumstances. This environment required careful scheduling of the computer to maximize throughput.

Today, computing power is generally more readily available because of dramatic price/performance improvements of vendors. Technological improvements in software have simplified operations. Memory sizes have increased in large multiples, and memory is normally supplemented with a virtual-memory technique. Control programs provide job queuing and dynamic allocation of CPU and peripheral resources. And today's installations process a significantly larger number of jobs.

The effect of all this is to substantially change the requirements of scheduling methodologies. Previously, scheduling was aimed at precisely planning the use of the computer resource. Today, if capacity is planned properly, this objective is of much less importance. In fact, an installation is probably better off to let the system schedule itself under control program parameters and to concentrate on controlling the flow of work to and from the system.

Job Information Prerequisites

The fundamental prerequisite for scheduling is to establish the time requirements of every job processed—that is, "due in" and "due out" time, or the "normal turnaround." The computer services group must negotiate these schedules with the user. Whenever possible, each job should have a predictable frequency—daily, weekly, monthly, the fifteenth of each month, or whatever—to facilitate schedule planning. But computer services must press users to commit themselves to regular schedules and to discipline themselves to follow these schedules. The schedule should state precisely the day and time the input is due to computer services and the day and time output is due to the users.

Keeping in mind that schedule performance is an important aspect of its customer service objectives, the computer services group must consider recovery time during production as part of its agreement. The more time that can be allowed between due-in and due-out dates, the better. A minimum standard is to schedule total job time as double the normal processing time. This allows for peak volumes for the job and peak loads in general, as well as recovery time.

Occasionally, certain jobs are not needed at any regular frequency. These are special-request jobs, which are not a part of the schedule until requested by the user. Schedules for these jobs are negotiated as normal turnaround. Because of the possibility that peaking in special requests will disrupt the entire schedule, longer total job times should be required for these jobs. Twenty-four hours or more is not unreasonable as a guideline.

Once jobs are inventoried and schedules are negotiated, a data file of scheduling information is developed. Figure 6-1 is a sample form called an EDP job process sheet. A form is completed for every application processed by the installation. Descriptor information is completed at the top, and each job and its number are indicated within the first two columns. The frequency code—D for daily, and so on—is listed under the column marked "F," and the schedule for the job under the column so headed. A step number is assigned sequentially for every processing step in the job. A step is defined as whenever a job moves from one processing location to another. These locations are called work centers. The work center name for each step is noted. The next three columns provide descriptive informa-

DATE ______ APPLICATION ______ PAGE ____ OF ____

JOB NAME	JOB NO.	F	SCHEDULE		STEP NO.	WORK CENTER	COMPUTER PROCESSING						KEYPUNCH		OUTPUT				WORK CENTER SCHED.	
			In	Out			Mem.	Tape 7	Tape 9	Disk	Printer	Run	Volume	Media	B	D	C	Time	In	Out

Figure 6-1. EDP job process sheet.

tion on the work center. Only one of these is ever completed for a single processing step. The computer processing data vary according to the configuration and technology, but generally describe the computer requirements of the job. The keypunch data indicate normal volume for keypunch steps and note the media when options are available. Checks are made under the appropriate "Output" columns to indicate whether the outputs are to be bursted (B) or decollated (D) or whether control balancing (C) is required, and the normal time for these activities is indicated. In the last double column, the schedule for each processing step is entered. The due-in time of the first step is the due-in time for the job, and the due-out time for the last step is the due-out time for the job. This job process sheet defines the steps as well as the normal schedule for the job.

Scheduling for Work Centers

Work centers can be defined according to the processing needs of the installation. A work center is designated for every major function in the processing cycle. There are a minimum of four work centers required for most installations. A receiving center receives work, checks for completeness, performs any stamping or receipting desired, and follows up when input is not received on schedule. A keypunch work center and a computer operations work center are needed too. An output work center that prepares reports and dispatches them to users is the other basic requirement. Figures 6-2 through 6-5 are examples of work center schedule forms. Each has been designed to accommodate the needs of the center. The forms are self-explanatory in relation to Figure 6-2.

Additional work centers can be defined according to needs. An installation that does formal setup or packaging of computer jobs may want a setup work center. A department that does extensive balancing would want a balance control work center. Special forms can be developed for each, or a multipurpose form can be designed. Note that "Due In" and "Due Out" columns are common to all. Work centers should be determined before designing and completing job process sheets.

Ongoing Scheduling

When work centers are organized, job process sheets are completed, and scheduling forms are available, the scheduling process

DATE ___/___/___

| JOB NO. | JOB NAME | INPUT DESCRIPTION | DUE IN TIME | | COMMENTS |
			SCHEDULED	ACTUAL	

Figure 6-2.   Daily receiving schedule.

___/___/___
DATE

JOB NO.	JOB NAME	VOLUME	MEDIA			DUE IN		DUE OUT		COMMENTS
			Card	7T	9T	Sched	Act.	Sched	Act.	

Figure 6-3. Keypunch daily schedule.

JOB NO.	JOB NAME	SET UP	SYSTEM	NORMAL TIME	PARTITION/ PRIORITY	DUE IN		DUE OUT		COMMENTS
						Sched.	Act.	Sched.	Act.	

DATE ___/___/___

Figure 6-4. EDP computer processing schedule.

___/___/___
DATE

JOB NO.	JOB NAME	OUTPUT DESCRIPTION	SPECIAL			DUE OUT TIME		COMMENTS
			B	D	C	Scheduled	Actual	

Figure 6-5. Daily output schedule.

can begin. The individual responsible for schedule planning uses the job process sheets as an information source and posts all steps for each job to be included in the schedule for the appropriate work center. Then the steps within each work center are sequenced, in order of due-in times on the schedule forms.

From a practical standpoint, it is neither feasible nor necessary to completely rebuild a schedule each day. For installations with a predominance of daily work, a daily schedule is prepared as a basis for every day's operation. This is adjusted each day to reflect special-request and other irregular jobs. Other shops may want a day-of-the-week schedule as a basis, or some other scheme, depending on the work load. However they are prepared, schedules will require periodic maintenance.

Once the schedule is completed, it is issued to the appropriate computer services personnel. Someone in production control should be designated on each shift to monitor the schedule. In larger shops, this is a full-time schedule expediter. The scheduler monitors progress at each work center, expedites jobs as required, and adjusts schedules as necessary. Each work center supervisor is accountable for processing according to the schedule and for reporting expected slippages to the scheduler.

Computer services management is vitally interested in information regarding late user outputs. The daily output schedule readily provides statistical data for this purpose. For daily problem solving, a report form such as the one in Figure 6-6 is quite useful. On it, all jobs in arrears as of a certain time each day are listed.

Scheduling effectiveness is critical to the performance of any computer services group. Not only is it required to meet the customer service objectives, but it also provides a better-planned and smoother operation that uses resources efficiently. Therefore, comprehensive scheduling will in the long run minimize resource requirements.

This overview requires thorough consideration and detailed procedures before implementation. Because of the vital nature of this activity and its potential complexity, it may well be necessary to seek outside assistance if there is no in-house expertise. The basic concepts of this technique have long been used in manufacturing, but also by some data processing installations. A reputable consultant should be considered.

96

____/____/____
DATE

JOB NO.	JOB NAME	SCHEDULED		REVISED SCHEDULE		EXPLANATION OF DELAY
		DATE	TIME	DATE	TIME	

Figure 6-6. EDP daily status report form.

TAPE LIBRARY PROCEDURES

No less important than scheduling methodology are the techniques relating to data file control. Since disk data are normally backed up on tapes, these procedures normally address tape handling. Because tapes are usually stored in a room known as a library, tape-handling procedures are often referred to as tape library procedures.

Tape library procedures need not be especially complex to be effective. But ineffective tape library controls can be the cause of inefficient operation at the least, and disaster at the worst. One company learned the cost of neglect in the tape library when all copies of a key master file were inadvertently scratched. The cost of manual reconstruction was $500,000. Even if an installation does nothing else with respect to controls, it must establish procedures for the tape library.

The tape library itself should be considered before developing tape control procedures. A tape library is not an open rack of tapes in the corner of the computer room. Smaller installations can purchase a safe designed for storing computer tapes. This should have the proper fire rating and secure locks. Larger installations can build a room of appropriate size for use as a tape library. Walls should be fire-rated and extend from building floor to building ceiling, not just from raised floor to a suspended ceiling, to isolate it from fire hazards.

Fire prevention systems, discussed earlier, are most important to the tape library. The library should be located within the computer room for operational convenience, and its access should be restricted. In larger installations where a tape librarian can be justified, not even computer operators are allowed access to the tape library. And by all means, the library is backed up at another site outside the building.

Tape library control procedures should perform three main functions:

1. Control the location of every generation of every file.
2. Control the usage of each reel of tape.
3. Organize the tapes so that reels are readily located.

Setting Up the Tape Library

Tape files are retained for several "generations." Each time a file is updated, the previous version is kept for some period as backup. Normally, tape retention requirements are stated in terms of the minimum number of generations of the file to be kept. Retentions vary according to recovery requirements of the particular application, but at least three generations of each file must be retained—the oldest at the remote storage location, and the two most current in the tape library. Keeping current versions in the remote vault would clearly simplify recovery in a disaster situation, but the problems caused in day-to-day operations by having only one version in the library don't warrant this extra measure of protection. The most effective method for controlling tapes and data is to file physical volumes in numerical sequence according to preassigned numbers and establish a cross-indexing system to control the use and location of the volumes. This is like the approach of neighborhood libraries.

In order to implement this type of procedure, several preliminary steps are necessary. Each reel must be designated with a permanent volume serial number. These can be assigned sequentially, the key requirement being that there is no duplication of numbers. Tape racks are also serially numbered in the same manner, with each slot having a unique number. Tapes are then filed by serial number in the corresponding slot. This allows for ease of location of tapes. File description labels should be obtained. All labels are available from vendors of data processing accessories. Finally, forms must be designed to use in recording file assignments and tape location and usage.

Figures 6-7 and 6-8 are suitable forms for tape library controls. During the implementation of tape library procedures, a file control card (Figure 6-7) is prepared for every data file to be retained. When the file is first created, a card is completed with the general information at the top. A unique file number is assigned to each file, using an alphanumeric number to avoid confusing file and reel numbers. The program number of the program creating the file is noted in the space designated "Created." The file name and application are written in the appropriate area, and the media designation can be used if the installation chooses to also use the system for primary disk files. Retentions are normally stated in generations, but in some cases, dates or time periods might be used. A reel control card (Figure 6-8)

| File # _____ | | File Name _____ | | | Application _____ | |
| Created _____ | | Media _____ | | | Retention _____ | |
Work Date	REEL Numbers				Assigned by	Scratch Date	Approved	Special Retention

Figure 6-7. A file control card.

Volume Number ______________ Date Purchased ______________ Vendor ______________

Date	File #	Released by	Date	File #	Released by

Figure 6-8. A reel control card.

is prepared for every physical volume when it enters the tape library. Statistical information can be used for quality control programs and be as extensive as the installation desires.

Three categories of control cards are maintained. One category comprises all file control cards, which are in sequential order by file number. Reel control cards are separated into two categories: control cards for tapes that are currently assigned and retained (these cards are also in sequential order), and control cards for tapes that are available for usage. The reel control cards in the latter category need not be in any special order.

Tape Library Operation

When a job is being set up for processing, all pertinent tape files are identified from the application documentation or special job setup documentation if available. The file control cards are pulled for those tape files. Tape input files are identified from the file control card, and the physical volumes are located in the racks. The appropriate reel control cards for output tapes are pulled from the scratch group. The file and reel control cards are updated. The file control card is completed with the work date of the job, the reel numbers the file will reside on, and the initials of the individual assigning reels. The date and the file number being assigned to the reel are indicated on the appropriate reel control card. The tapes are pulled, the output tapes are labeled, and the cards are refiled. The tapes are now ready for processing.

Periodically, file control cards should be reviewed for tape volumes available for scratching. The current tapes being held are compared to the retention. Extra generations can be scratched unless the need for special retention is noted in the far right column. When tapes are scratched, the date is listed under "Scratch Date," and the initials of the person approving the action are noted. The reel control card for the volume is pulled, and the initials of the person scratching are noted under the "Released By" column. The labels are removed from the physical volume, and the cards are refiled, with the reel control card going to the scratch category.

The file control cards are also used to determine which tapes should be moved to remote storage. The card is reviewed, and appropriate volumes are noted on a list of tapes to be moved. It is beneficial to note this action with a code such as R on the file control card under "Special Retention" to prevent someone later fruitlessly looking for the tape. Reel control cards should be periodically reviewed. Statistical data, plus a review of the number of times the reel has been used, as indicated on the card, will determine when tapes should be reconditioned or purged from the library. This will help maintain high tape quality.

For installations with a large library of tapes, the clerical work involved in this procedure can be significant. Several software packages are available to perform this function, and some are very good. The advantage of these is not only time savings but greater accuracy, as less manual recording reduces the chance of error. Whichever approach is chosen, the need for accuracy cannot be stressed enough. If a full-time librarian is not justified, one person should still be designated with this responsibility, as opposed to everyone in the data center participating. In either case, the individual chosen should be a person of proven dependability who is meticulous about detail. Even though the duties are somewhat routine, the responsibility is tremendous, and the person should be compensated accordingly.

INPUT AND OUTPUT CONTROLS

Sufficient input and output controls are also required in computer services. The scope of input controls is to ensure that all required input is received, that it is received on time, and that it is complete. Output controls are the reciprocal—they ensure that all input is dispatched, is on time, and is complete. The scheduling system provides part of the required control. The daily receiving schedule shown in Figure 6-2 and the daily output schedule in Figure 6-5 provide a control vehicle to follow up on the timely processing of input and output. Implementation of additional input and output controls is necessary to ensure quality service.

Input controls will vary by job. If the input is a reel of tape, properly noting this as part of the description on the daily receiving schedule is sufficient. However, when multiple batches are received for keypunching, additional procedures are necessary. Computer services should not do detailed reconciliation of input, but a transmittal sheet indicating the number of batches can provide a mechanism for a quick check. Normally, these input procedures are considered as part of the application design, but the computer services group suffers the immediate headaches of reruns and customer complaints resulting from improper processing, so it should review these procedures carefully. Perhaps computer services can outline control standard requirements to be used as part of the application development standards of the EDP department.

Output controls are also ultimately the responsibility of computer services. Fundamentally, output controls ensure that the work is accurate and complete and that the general appearance is acceptable. As on the input side, certain control totals should be available to computer services to evaluate processing. These can be either dollar totals or record counts, and they should assure that all input has been processed and the proper files were used in processing. Again, detailed reconciliation is up to the user. Someone should review output reports and ensure that all reports are accounted for, that the number of copies is correct, and that the general quality in terms of print readability and order of reports is sufficient. A convenient method to provide this control is to develop a checklist for the larger applications to use as a guide for quality review. Each checklist can be given a code number, which would be included on the appropriate line of the daily output schedule to indicate that a checklist review is required.

The basic control techniques for input and output are relatively simple and consume little time and effort. Their simplicity, not their unimportance, is the reason for the brevity of the discussion. Customer service is the top priority of the computer services group. Technical competence and sophistication is for naught if the reports that go to the user are of low quality. Therefore, EDP management must recognize this need and ensure that appropriate procedures are developed and used.

TELEPROCESSING DEMANDS

To a large extent, the controls discussed deal with batch applications. Teleprocessing applications create a different set of problems.

For an on-line system to be of value to a user, uptime must be very high. This requirement puts the standards of reliability much higher than ever before. EDP management must be aware of the reasons that user time is lost and take preventive measures.

The first problem is simply one of scheduling. The computer must be available when teleprocessing systems are scheduled to begin. Also, batch update applications that generate files for teleprocessing systems must be processed in time for on-line systems. Software development and change management techniques have already been discussed. Hardware reliability must be maintained, as discussed in Chapter 8. Reliability is a function of minimizing the occurrences of downtime as well as minimizing the recovery time when failures occur, so attention must be given to the training required by the operator to handle these special problems and the recovery procedures provided. Procedures must be complete in terms of the types of failures addressed and the detailed recovery steps for each type.

Teleprocessing systems create one additional new problem for computer services. Besides the requirement for reliability, on-line systems must maintain adequate response time to be of value to users. Response time is defined as the elapsed time between terminal requests for information and receipt of that information. Response time initially is a function of the proper design of the software, the communications network, and the host configuration. Assuming the adequacy of these designs, computer services has an ongoing duty to guard against periodic degradation of response time.

Response time degradation can occur due to hardware and software failures, improper multiprogramming, improper use of shared disk devices in a multi-CPU environment, or many other reasons. The first step in controlling response time is to establish procedures to minimize degradation. These are standards for multiprogramming in the on-line environment and similar preventive measures. They should be developed in consultation with the technical support group.

Once preventive procedures are developed, recovery procedures are also needed. The situation here is more complicated, because it is not always obvious to the computer operator when response time has degraded. The user will eventually report the problem, but it is amazing how long many users wait before complaining. A manager of a department that utilized a teleprocessing system once seriously reported a 45-minute response time to the computer services group of his company. This was not true. Such obviously erroneous information can be misleading and hamper problem solving.

Some companies have tailored teleprocessing software to provide response time statistics automatically. This method can be especially effective when intelligent terminals or intelligent remote-control units are used. Ideally, the response time would include a comparison to a standard and provide a warning message on the console when a problem is detected. Whatever the exact measurement method, procedures for detecting response time problems and resolving them must be developed.

A teleprocessing environment creates a host of new problems. Shops with large on-line systems should consider appointing specialists responsible for maintaining network hardware and controlling reliability and response time.

PROBLEM CONTROL

Chapter 4 reviewed issues relating to problem control in the EDP department. A procedure for recording, reporting, and following up on problems as well as providing summary reporting for review by the change management committee is needed. Problems can range from reports of poor print quality to major software and hardware malfunctions. Reports can be generated by users, a programmer who encounters a compiler bug, or virtually anyone associated with data processing.

Many people report problems and many different EDP groups are involved in problem solving, depending on the nature of the problem. Because of this, it is natural to be inclined toward multiple problem control systems. When each group in the organization has its own problem reporting procedure, it is more difficult to control problems, a risk of duplicate efforts is created, and consolidating reporting is more difficult. Designating one individual for problem control will be more efficient. Because most problems in some manner affect computer services' ability to respond to user production needs, this group is the logical one to handle this responsibility.

The natural person to assign problem control to is the individual assigned to customer service in the production control section. All problem reports should be directed to this individual, regardless of who reports the problem or who will be required to resolve it. This person must be very service-oriented, have a good understanding of the responsibility, assignments, and operation of the entire EDP department, and be the type who is tenacious about following up on reported problems.

A multiple-part problem report is a very effective base for the problem control system. Figure 6-9 is a sample of a trouble report. The top part of the sheet is for descriptive information required to document the problem. The area in the middle describes the problem in detail. The next section provides data on who reported the problem, to whom it was referred, and what the time requirements are for resolution. The trouble report should be a three-part carbon form. It is always completed by the individual responsible for customer service. The forms are serially numbered. Each problem report should be recorded by serial number, and each number should be accounted for to ensure that no report is lost. Two copies are sent to the person identified under "Person Notified," who is to resolve the situation. This may be a vendor service engineer, an application programmer, a systems programmer, or someone in computer services. The customer service representative maintains the third copy of the form in a tickler file for followup if the problem is not resolved promptly.

The person receiving the report investigates the problem and resolves it as quickly as possible and in accordance with special requirements if possible. When it is resolved, he completes the "Corrective Action" section and sends it to the customer service representative, who closes it out from the open file. Closed reports are maintained in another file for future statistical analysis.

To facilitate further control, a summary reporting system is required. A format of a weekly summary is shown in Figure 6-10. This report is prepared as of a certain time and day each week by the customer service representative and distributed to the installation management committee as well as to appropriate section managers. At its weekly meeting, the committee reviews outstanding problems

Problem Type _____	Date Reported _____
Reported By _____	Reported To _____

HARDWARE PROBLEM

_____CPU   DEVICE # _____   LOCATION _____
_____DISK   TIME UP _____   METER _____
_____TAPE   TIME DOWN _____   METER _____
_____PRINTER   TIME LOST _____   METER _____

SOFTWARE   DIAGNOSTICS (Describe and Attach)

_____CONTROL SOFTWARE
_____PACKAGE SOFTWARE
_____APPLICATION PROGRAM
_____OTHER

Problem Description_____

_____

_____

_____

_____

_____

Prepared by	Person Notified	Date Required

CORRECTIVE ACTION_____

_____

_____

_____

_____

Figure 6-9. EDP trouble report form.

Figure 6-10. Weekly EDP trouble report recap.

Week Ending _____

Problem #	Date Reported	Description	Date Required	Responsi-bility	Status

Figure 6-11. Problem history summary form.

Problem Classification	Type	Number		
		This Week	Year to Date	Last Year
Hardware Failures	CPU			
	Tapes			
	Disks			
	Printers			
System Software	Control Program			
	TP Monitor			
	Cobol Compiler			
Operations Errors	Poor Print Quality			
	Copies Missing			
	Report Missing			
Application Aborts	General Ledger			
	Inventory Control			
	Payroll			

and ensures that proper action is taking place for each and resolution efforts are coordinated.

In addition to expediting the resolution of open problems, the installation committee is also interested in identifying problem trends and formulating policies and defining programs to address repetitive problems. Figure 6-11 is a sample of a summary statistical report, which should also be prepared for the committee on a weekly basis. The problem classifications can, of course, be defined according to the needs of the department. Also, data on responsibility might be useful. The required form would follow the same basic format, but the classifications would identify groups and sections of the EDP department that were responsible for the failures.

The effectiveness of this procedure depends on developing the appropriate attitudes of all members of the EDP staff, beginning with the management team. Customer service objectives dictate a need for a prompt and thorough response to problem reports. And the ongoing analysis of problem trends must be complete and imaginative.

CONTROLLING OPERATIONAL RESOURCES

Chapter 9 is dedicated to the very important subject of EDP planning. Although it is not appropriate to discuss matters relating to planning methodology here, there are some planning issues that are relevant as a conclusion to this chapter on computer services control techniques.

Planning of EDP resources normally addresses user requirements, the hardware necessary, and the systems development staff needed to execute the plan. All too often, other computer services resources are not considered as a part of intermediate- and long-range planning. Plans for the computer services physical facility, staff, and other needs are normally analyzed only on a one-year term as a part of annual budgeting, if at all. But facility upgrades take long lead times, contract terms for all hardware and miscellaneous equipment purchases must be considered in view of long-range requirements, and staffing changes can necessitate careful advanced planning. If these issues are not adequately considered, chaos can develop.

Frequently, computer rooms are too jammed as a result of inadequate planning of facility needs. Often there isn't enough room for chairs, far less for adequate work staging and control stations. Many installations have suffered difficulties as a result of the environment being insufficient because hardware was increased. Other installations operate with improper key conversion equipment because someone signed a long-term contract without proper forethought. These problems and others necessitate that computer services management carefully plan resources.

Once the hardware plan is completed, the staff plan must be developed. The basis for staff planning is the development of "typical" schedules for periods in the future, using the scheduling methods discussed earlier in the chapter. Admittedly, this process requires some guess work, but estimates and assumptions made in this effort should be at least accurate enough to show growth trends. Once the schedules are completed, reasonably accurate staffing estimates can be prepared. Staffing levels will most often dictate the number of keypunches and other types of special equipment.

When the staff and equipment requirements are known, the facility requirements can be determined relatively easily. The square footage and layout of each section must be determined. Raised-floor needs for computer hardware, temperature and humidity standards, and security systems designs then follow. It cannot be overemphasized how important attention to facility planning can be. An inadequate facility is just plainly detrimental to computer services operations.

Once the plan is completed, it should periodically be reviewed to determine the need for updates. Also, computer services management would be wise to provide some buffer in the plan. Don't work too closely in planning space and other facility requirements. Chances are extra space will eventually be used, and it is cheaper to build growth space during initial construction than to try to add it later. Be careful when negotiating long-term contracts for equipment. Don't be enticed by lower monthly charges to the point of omitting a thorough analysis of the probability of obsolesence.

111

-7-

Managing Human Resources

THE EDP department uses two basic resources to do its job. The first is its people. Trite as it may seem to say, the people in any organization are its greatest asset. The other important resource is the computer hardware. Managing these resources is the most important function of EDP management. The issues of planning, organization, and control discussed in preceding and succeeding chapters are really aimed at optimizing the utilization and performance of personnel and hardware resources. There are additional techniques more directly concerned with these resources. Some of these are general management tools applicable to any type of organization, and some are peculiar to the EDP organization. Taking matters in the order of importance, the personnel management approach is discussed first in this chapter, and the next chapter concludes with topics relevant to managing the hardware resource.

EMPLOYER–EMPLOYEE PERSPECTIVES

Many aspects of the employer–employee relationship must be analyzed in order to develop personnel management policies. EDP management must understand personnel in the EDP job market and develop an environment that is attractive for recruiting. Once the EDP department makes itself attractive, it must develop recruiting techniques that will identify the best candidates. The EDP department needs to define challenging, fulfilling jobs with the opportunity for career development. And it must measure the performance of personnel in their positions and must evaluate their potential for advancement. In summary, the successful EDP department must provide an opportunity for satisfying careers for its employees and, at the same time, be demanding in terms of performance expectations. Being the most attractive employer in the area is of little use if the company doesn't use its personnel resources well. And having the highest employment and performance standards is useless if the company cannot attract capable people.

To set the stage for the discussion, it is useful to briefly ponder today's EDP employment market and consider its problems. To be very general, the most obvious characteristic of the market is that there is an extreme shortage of qualified EDP technicians relative to the aggregate demand. The phenomenal growth of EDP departments over the last few years continues to outstrip the supply of personnel. The competitiveness has accelerated EDP salaries, often faster than general business growth, creating internal problems of equity in some companies. The EDP career professional has become very mobile in terms of company and geography. He has many employment opportunities.

How do EDP managers perceived the job market? Some feel that it is overpriced. They perceive that many EDP technicians are intent on being thought of and treated as professionals but do not want to accept responsibilities as professionals. Complaints that there are a large number of incompetents in the market are often heard. Technically qualified individuals are often thought of as undependable and lacking loyalty and a business sense.

EDP professionals also have their complaints about employers. They often feel that management creates a chaotic work environment. They perceive management as being uninformed technically and unrealistic in expectations, and they complain of prolonged periods of long work weeks in many installations. EDP professionals often feel that their professional opinions are not given enough

113

consideration and that companies classify them as technicians, making the EDP department a dead end in terms of career growth.

Of course, the environment is different in individual companies, but there is probably some truth to all the preceding statements in most firms. EDP departments that are perfect employers don't exist, and there are few that seem to have a fulfilling environment in the long run for its employees. On the other hand, there are individuals in the market who call themselves EDP professionals but are marginally competent and others who should be classified as unemployable.

This situation is enough to cause some employers to abandon the whole EDP effort, especially if they give the problems of maintaining an EDP staff much thought. Obviously, this is not viable as an alternative for most companies, so the EDP manager must find a way to operate effectively in this labor market. In the long run, participation in professional groups that advocate upgrading of standards, certification and licensing, and things of this nature might be helpful. But obviously, no short-term solution will result from this. The EDP manager must proceed with the assumption that there are enough qualified professionals in his market area to staff his department, even if there aren't enough to go around in the overall market. His challenge is to provide the proper environment to get more than his fair share.

MOTIVATORS OF EDP PROFESSIONALS

Before designing the job package that will be successful, the EDP manager must understand what it is candidates are looking for. When analyzing employee motivation, generalizations are difficult, and the experts certainly don't always agree. Although motivational theory is beyond the scope of this book, a few generalizations are worthwhile.

Regardless of what researchers say and managers conclude about money, it is an important motivator. The least we can say is that disappointing a person's economic aspirations is a demotivator. If you don't think this is true, create an "ideal" work environment and try to hire experienced technicians at $10,000 below the yearly market salaries. Today's inflationary economy contributes to money becoming a more important employment consideration. Also, equity in salaries is a measure of the sense of fairness of the company.

But don't think an EDP team can merely be bought. EDP professionals are normally attracted to stay in the business because of certain characteristics of EDP work that are harmonious with their abilities and personalities. The top-notch professional is attracted by opportunities to learn on a continuous basis and to be constantly challenged in respect to his skills. He wants the satisfaction of being a part of successful projects. He is interested in his long-range future.

So the EDP department that wants to attract top-notch professionals must start with a competitive and comprehensive package of compensation. The process of salary determination is more complex than merely ordering EDP salaries with the rest of the company. Because a great deal of outside recruiting will be necessary, the salary levels of the market must be considered. EDP professionals are not restricted to careers in any given industry, so the salary survey will have to cross industry lines. Benefits analysis— insurance, vacation, pensions, and so on—must follow a similar pattern.

The need for competitive compensation is as important in small installations as in large ones. Many small shops feel that they are not as complex because of their size, therefore they don't have to pay the salaries of the larger companies to get suitable talent. This is a totally erroneous assumption. Although the volumes in small shops are obviously lower, it does not necessarily follow that complexity is less. Some small shops have in fact more complex requirements for like applications than larger ones. Lower salaries will yield commensurate talent in the long run and leave little hope for a successful EDP endeavor. Some companies would argue that the company salary structure just can't support competitive EDP compensation. This contention must be critically examined. If it is true, the company should seriously question its intention to build an EDP department and reconsider other options such as service bureaus.

Once the compensation package is tied together, the company

must have an EDP plan to discuss with experienced candidates. Today's job seekers are no longer interested in merely discussing the initial assignment; they also want a preview of subsequent prospects. The EDP manager who cannot discuss future plans will be at a decided disadvantage in recruiting discussions. The content and technology anticipated for the projects are also important. EDP professionals are seeking challenging application opportunities and state-of-the-art technology. No one would suggest that new technology be adopted merely to please prospective employees (although this benefit should be an intangible in the analysis of new technologies); nevertheless, an installation using obsolete equipment and software must recognize it has a serious shortcoming in the eyes of prospects.

More and more, EDP professionals are thinking about their careers in longer-range terms. This almost inevitably emerges in the interview process. The employer must show a commitment to policies and a history of examples of providing EDP personnel with career opportunities rather than merely technical positions. A policy of promotions from within the department for section and project manager positions is the first step. Providing opportunities for movement into user areas for more business-oriented people is another plus. Even cross-movement between EDP groups is attractive to some candidates. Each EDP department must customize career path plans to its own environment, but failure to be prepared to discuss the subject thoroughly is a significant detriment.

The work environment is also quite often important in attracting candidates. The corporate climbers of previous years who will work any hours in any location in order to achieve career advancement seem to be disappearing from the scene. Management is faced with a generation of job seekers who are much more preoccupied with the quality of their lives and are less willing to accept assignments without question. These characteristics are reflected in many parts of today's society. The employer with a location that minimizes commute time has an advantage. When jobs are plentiful, why should an employee commute two hours each day when there is an opportunity around the corner? A large number of today's candidates are reluctant to accept a position where long hours and weekend work are a way of life, no matter what opportunities are offered. The company must package the work environment accordingly. Location is often not flexible, but management must consider the company's location and compensate for problems. For example, if the company is in a high-crime area, it should develop programs such as parking-lot security.

Staffing should be adequate and objectives realistic to avoid the round-the-clock pressures for individuals. Certainly, few professions offer regular 8:30 to 5:00 work hours, but some reasonable limits have to be set. A flexitime schedule should be evaluated for the systems groups. The program allows individuals to set their own work schedules, within certain guidelines, to achieve the standard work week. This approach entrusts the individual with the professional responsibility he seeks. It also is a way for employers in the center of large urban areas to allow employees an opportunity to avoid rush-hour congestion. The advantages to the employee are numerous, but don't jump in blindly; there are those who will take advantage of the freedom.

The physical environment in which people work is also a significant factor. The candidate interviewed in a location that looks like a factory will not be too impressed. Cramped quarters, inadequate work and filing space, poor lighting, and a generally unattractive environment are not only a detriment to hiring but are a negative influence on productivity. Modest investments in the facility can pay big dividends.

To many prospective employees, the impressions of the people they will work for and with are as vital as anything. They are looking for managers they can enjoy working with and from whom they can learn. Weak managers, of course, produce many problems, with recruiting being another important one. The company should put its best foot forward in terms of the people who do the interviewing. Interviewers must be honest with the candidate, although they certainly must sell the department's advantages. Sometimes, allowing the candidate to talk with a potential peer helps increase credibility, but care must be taken to select the right employee for the peer interview. In essence, be positive but don't make absurd promises that everyone knows can't be kept.

In summary, the attractive company is one that has a competitive compensation package, provides challenging work assignments in

117

the short run and career opportunities in the long run, offers an attractive work environment from several standpoints, and presents a talented, people-oriented management team. This company is in a good position to attract the cream of the EDP labor market, because unfortunately not too many companies provide all these advantages. So, if the company has designed its organization this way, it has the right to expect high-quality professionals and should settle for nothing less. Under no circumstances should EDP managers get into the trap of becoming so preoccupied with the shortage of candidates that they allow the prospective employee to interview the company. Once a company has established its credentials as a good employer, it's entitled to demand that the candidate sell himself.

LOCATING AND RECRUITING CANDIDATES

Dropping back a step, the company must first locate individuals seeking opportunities. For the typical organization, personal referrals can be the best source of talent. With all the dialog between EDP personnel, chances are that some of the current employees have friends who are interested in the right opportunity. Good employees will give amazingly honest evaluations of former associates. Agencies are valuable in finding candidates, but the agency chosen should also be interviewed. Make sure the one selected understands the EDP business and provides more of a service than photocopying resumes. There is clearly a difference in the quality of service provided by various agencies. You may try direct advertising, but it doesn't seem to be too fruitful except for a few larger corporations with a strong public image.

However candidates are recruited, the qualifications for each position should be spelled out. The list should be realistic. Don't look for someone with technical experience not needed, or for somebody with management experience for nonmanagement positions. There are still a lot of talented non-degreed candidates in the market, so don't automatically eliminate them. On the other side, not everyone with an advanced degree will get results, so don't be sold on this alone.

118

Candidate Screening

Once the company's employment package is complete, job qualifications are known, and the top candidates are selected, the very difficult screening process must be undertaken. Basically, the process is intended to identify those individuals who have the skills, attitudes, and personality to fit into the organization and make substantial contributions. Sounds simple, but it's not. Even the most experienced interviewers are going to make some mistakes.

There are two basic screening tools available: interviewing and background checking. Some managers feel that checking references given by the candidate is useless because he will obviously never give a reference who would not provide a glowing report. But it is startling how many negative things are sometimes said by a reference supplied by the candidate. Of course, the opinion of a current employee can be invaluable on candidates personally referred by that employee. Checking former employers can often be futile because many companies are reluctant to give detailed references, but it is worth trying. When checking previous employers, try to avoid the screen of the personnel department and get right to the supervisor or manager for whom the candidate worked. Personal contacts of both the hiring company and the employment agency can also yield relevant information. College transcripts are useless for all but the very inexperienced entry-level candidate. Besides, grade averages are not necessarily a valid predictor of performance on the job.

The other tool of screening is the employment interview. After the candidate is presented with the advantages of employment, the interviewing process should be directed toward evaluating him. Given that no one has perfect insight, it is advantageous to have more than one person interview the candidate. This can be overdone, though, so be cautious—whatever approach is taken, don't give the impression that committee decisions prevail. The purpose of multiple interviews is to get multiple opinions, so some overlap of topic areas is acceptable, but interview sessions should not be purely repetitive. It is a good idea to have each interviewer concentrate on specific areas.

The interview process must cover several subjects. Technical know-how is obviously important. The candidate's experience with project control and other techniques and his attitude toward them are important for positions in the systems groups. Judgments about personality fit are essential but have to be more rational than "like" and "dislike" pronouncements. An appraisal of how flexible the candidate will be in accepting company methods is necessary. And finally, the career objectives of the candidate must be evaluated in light of the character of the company.

Interviewing techniques and skills must be acquired, and professional instruction should be considered. However, there are certain principles that should be used. First of all, be prepared for the interview. Second, do whatever possible to make the candidate feel at ease. Most people have some degree of anxiety in the interview situation. Start out slowly, have a cup of coffee, show him around the department and let him relax. Don't start off grilling him about achievements. The objective is to identify the right candidate, not to overlook a good one because he is nervous and intimidated. And, by all means, one interviewer at a time.

The best interviewing approach is to get the candidate to talk about his experiences, as opposed to going through a checklist of questions concerning technical areas. Get specific about what he has done. For example, if he worked on an inventory control project, find out exactly what his duties were. Have him comment on successes and failures. Find out what he felt he learned from the assignment. If his resume lists certain skills, determine exactly where he got them. Often a candidate will list a programming language, technique, or other experience to which he had only the most limited exposure. In areas where the interviewer is extremely well versed, he may want to ask questions that require thoughtful answers. For example, candidates who profess expertise in project control techniques could be asked to give their opinion on the fundamental requirements of a project control procedure. Don't ask obscure details that can easily be looked up in a work environment. The idea is to find out what the candidate really understands and how significant his experience has been.

When interviewing and history checking is completed, a decision must be reached. By all means, do this promptly—don't expect a top-notch person to wait forever. The interviewers should meet and discuss the candidate and evaluate all aspects. It must be determined if he has the skills, attitude, and personality to fit in. This is judgmental, and people who have the final say should be those responsible for the area to which the candidate would be assigned.

There are a few warning signals that must be observed. Watch out for the job hopper. If an individual has moved around a lot, there is no reason to think that he will stay in the newest position for an extended period. Find out why the candidate left previous jobs, especially if there is a history of lateral moves. When an individual shows many years with one company, but virtually no career growth, there may be a reason. Out-of-town candidates can be attractive, but the risk is high that they will someday return to their old location, for whatever reason. A company invests a lot of money in recruiting and orienting a new employee and therefore should try to weed out the short-termers.

Employee Orientation

Once the candidate is hired, the EDP manager must assimilate him into the organization. The size of the organization will usually dictate the formality of the orientation period. However presented, an orientation program should fully familiarize the employee with the business of the company and the plan of the EDP department. General administrative procedures, such as processing insurance claims, and EDP department procedures, such as test time scheduling, should be explained. The new employee should be shown all employee facilities and be introduced to key people he will be working with. Finally, his supervisor should present him with the job description for his position and review it with him. The employee should also be given direction on what is expected of him on initial assignments.

In-House Development Programs

Considering all the time and cost involved in recruiting, one might wonder why EDP departments don't develop in-house talent rather than endure this continuous struggle. The question is quite valid. Essentially, most departments have tight schedules and budget restrictions and therefore feel that they must get the most production out of each position. This means that experienced people are required. But no matter how good the screening process, some errors will be made. Some candidates won't work out. Others will eventually move to other opportunities. Couple this with the fact that most companies' manpower requirements grow, and there is no end in sight to the recruiting problem.

The answer is for EDP departments to begin developing their own resources. Special budget positions must be allowed for manpower development. Inexperienced college graduates with degrees in computer science and other fields can be hired and put into long-term development programs. Better yet, provide educational assistance to computer services personnel at the clerical level, along with a career path that leads to the systems and programming professions.

In the short run there is additional expense, because the EDP department will probably have to continue recruiting experienced people until the in-house pool develops. But in the long run, it will be cheaper. Also, the individuals will have more knowledge of the company from long-term experience, and, because of their seniority, have more at stake and be less likely to leave for another company. Barring a major economic collapse or technological breakthrough substantially reducing the number of technicians required in the EDP field—neither of which is likely in the near term—this appears to be the only way out of the supply/demand crisis and all its ramifications.

MAINTAINING THE RIGHT ENVIRONMENT

Once staffing is completed, by whatever method, the challenge for EDP management is to retain employees and maximize their productivity. This is a matter of motivating people, not coercing them. Again, motivational theory and a detailed employee relations analysis are beyond the scope of this book, but there are a few common complaints of EDP professionals and some approaches that can be considered. Assuming that screening procedures have been effective, the ensuing discussion presumes a quite competent staff.

All the programs outlined as part of the recruiting package are of course important on an ongoing basis. If the presentations regarding compensation packages, career opportunities, and job assignments turn out to not be true, turnover will start quickly. But there are other things that may become equally important in the relationship between employee and company.

Fortunately, items that are important to management are also important to really good staff members. Top-notch professionals like to get things done and done right. They are not happy when projects end in disaster or when they are moved from assignment to assignment without ever being allowed to finish anything. They are proud to be part of an EDP department that is, on the whole, performing well and has a good reputation. So, all the techniques which contribute to a well-run EDP department will contribute to improved morale and motivation of its employees, and this will continue to improve the performance of the department.

EDP professionals want to make an impact on the environment. Large shops in particular make the mistake of assigning people to a section or project and then giving them a small piece of that project to complete, with no chance to contribute to overall project direction. They are not given an adequate opportunity to express ideas on their own areas, far less on the department as a whole. The smart project manager will actively solicit the ideas and opinions of all the members of the project team. A section manager in computer services will give all members of the section a chance to comment on new procedures and other changes. Not only is this good for morale, but often some very good ideas can be obtained.

The broader the scope of personnel who are included in the EDP team, the better. Ideally, everyone in the EDP department feels that he is an important part. Management must provide opportunities on an ongoing basis. It can invite different individuals, on a rotating basis, to participate in the weekly meeting of the installation management committee. Ad hoc task forces formed to study and make recommendations on technical and even administrative problems are another way to get staff members involved. The planning process should include as many people as possible to achieve broad support for objectives and programs. Balance and perspective are the operative words here. People should be allowed to get involved.

However, it is by no means suggested that all decisions be made by vote or anything close. Just create an environment where people can have their ideas heard.

Management must also communicate with staffers. Areas to be included range from department objectives and plans to personnel changes such as promotions and reassignments. Many EDP departments become bogged down with activity and communicate on a need-to-know basis only, if that. EDP managers cannot expect their employees to care about the department as a whole if they don't give them information. The department rumor mill, normally a function of a lack of communication, not only consumes time but circulates misinformation that can be detrimental to morale. Bulletin board postings, special meetings, reports, and the like are all useful vehicles for communicating information. But there is no substitute for managers and supervisors talking to their people. Not only do managers communicate this way, but they get a chance to listen.

Policies of EDP management regarding personnel are important in the ongoing relationship. Certain restrictions on personnel are necessary, if for no other reason than to safeguard against the occasional goof-off. Overcontrolling lunch hour, relief periods, and rest-room breaks will cause resentment. This may seem obvious, but some managers try to do this. In the long run, project control reports and other types of performance measurement techniques will identify the slackers, and the cost of what they chisel in the meantime isn't worth eliminating an environment of professional freedom.

Some managers are all take and no give. They feel that even though an operator may have worked throughout a weekend conversion schedule, he must be docked according to the "book" for coming in a couple of hours late Monday morning. This subject is a matter of personal philosophy, but it seems common sense to allow some latitude in regulations. Each EDP manager should think about it before setting the climate for his area. Occasionally a manager is gifted with really good instincts about people and has good judgment without giving too much conscious thought to it. But most managers need to think about their behavior and policies and their long-range impact.

Employees usually know who among their peers is good and who is not. If performance is not measured accurately and fairly and action is not taken accordingly, motivation problems arise. Nothing can be more disgusting for a high-caliber employee than to have to work with a "dead head" who makes the employee's job tougher and to see nothing done about it by management.

Performance Appraisals

A good performance appraisal system rewards those who get results and penalizes those who don't. A well-designed performance appraisal also improves performance by defining realistic objectives that require stretching. It provides a means for identifying areas of improvement for an employee so that he may develop himself.

Many types of performance appraisal systems based on many different philosophies are available. The method should be carefully chosen. Systems that dictate a periodic review of performance and achievements without any prior understanding of objectives create a lot of problems, the most frequent one being the legitimate complaint that the employee didn't understand what he would be rated on. Approaches that are based on appraisal of skills and abilities such as planning, technical ability, personal hygiene, or whatever are worse than nothing.

The only effective system to measure personnel performance is one that requires employee and manager to mutually agree on performance objectives and calls for the performance to be measured against these objectives at some later date. The appraisal is essentially a determination of what was accomplished in respect to what was agreed upon. Figure 7-1 is a form that can be used as the foundation for an excellent performance appraisal system. The top of the first page is merely for statistical information. Normally, salary reviews are annual. One performance evaluation session is required to coincide with the salary review as a basis for salary action. Another is needed at the six-month interval between salary reviews to allow a time when performance issues are not clouded with the emotion of salary consideration.

Setting Performance Objectives

The first page of the form is the heart of the entire system. This page provides for the definition of performance objectives. These objectives should be stated as targets of performance for the major

Employee Name (Last, First, Initial)		Employee Number	Employment Date
Position Title		Department	
Current Evaluation Date	Last Evaluation Date	Salary Review Date	

PERFORMANCE PLANNING

RESPONSIBILITIES (KEY WORDS TO DESCRIBE THE MAJOR ELEMENTS OF THIS EMPLOYEE'S JOB.)	PERFORMANCE FACTORS AND/OR RESULTS TO BE ACHIEVED (A MORE SPECIFIC STATEMENT OF EMPLOYEE'S KEY RESPONSIBILITIES/GOALS EMPLOYEE CAN REASONABLY BE EXPECTED TO ACHIEVE IN COMING PERIOD.)

CHANGES IN PERFORMANCE PLAN (MAY BE RECORDED ANYTIME DURING THE APPRAISAL PERIOD.)

OPTIONAL ADDITIONAL PLANS (WHERE CONSIDERED APPROPRIATE BY MANAGER AND EMPLOYEE.)

Figure 7-1.   Performance appraisal form

126

PERFORMANCE EVALUATION						
ACTUAL ACHIEVEMENTS	LEVEL					OVERALL RATING
	10-9	8-7-6	5-4-3	2	1	(CONSIDERING ALL FACTORS, CHECK THE LEVEL OF ACHIEVEMENT WHICH BEST DESCRIBES THIS EMPLOYEE'S OVERALL PERFORMANCE DURING THE PAST PERIOD.)
						DISTINGUISHED □ 10 □ 9 RESULTS ACHIEVED VIRTUALLY CAN NOT BE IMPROVED.
						COMMENDABLE □ 8 □ 7 □ 6 RESULTS ACHIEVED CONSISTENTLY EXCEED THE REQUIREMENTS FOR THE JOB.
						COMPETENT □ 5 □ 4 □ 3 RESULTS ACHIEVED CONSISTENTLY MET THE REQUIREMENTS FOR THE JOB.
						FAIR □ 2 RESULTS ACHIEVED CAME CLOSE TO BEING ACCEPTABLE, BUT THE NEED FOR IMPROVEMENT IS RECOGNIZ-ABLE.
						MARGINAL □ 1 RESULTS ACHIEVED ARE CLEARLY BELOW THE ACCEPTABLE LEVEL. PROBATION RECOMMENDED.
						ADDITIONAL EVALUATION FACTORS **CONTINUING RESPONSIBILITIES** (RESPONSIBILITIES, NOT COVERED AT LEFT, TO BE CONSIDERED ONLY WHEN THEY HAVE HAD A SIGNIFICANT POSITIVE OR NEGATIVE EFFECT ON THE OVERALL PER-FORMANCE.)
						RELATIONSHIPS WITH OTHERS (Job Related) (SIGNIFICANT POSITIVE OR NEGATIVE INFLUENCE THIS EMPLOYEE HAS HAD ON THE PERFORMANCE OF OTHER EMPLOYEES.)
ADDITIONAL SIGNIFICANT ACCOMPLISHMENTS						

Figure 7-1.   Performance appraisal form (page 2).

127

COUNSELING SUMMARY

EMPLOYEE STRENGTHS   SUGGESTED IMPROVEMENTS

1. _____   1. _____

2. _____   2. _____

3. _____   3. _____

4.   4.

SIGNIFICANT INTERVIEW COMMENTS

(RECORD HERE ONLY THOSE ADDITIONAL SIGNIFICANT ITEMS BROUGHT UP DURING THE DISCUSSION BY EITHER YOU OR THE EMPLOYEE WHICH ARE NOT RECORDED ELSEWHERE IN THIS DOCUMENT.)

Manager's Signature	Print Name	Date of Interview

EMPLOYEE REVIEW

OPTIONAL COMMENTS: IF THE EMPLOYEE WISHES TO DO SO, ANY COMMENTS CONCERNING THE PERFORMANCE PLAN OR EVALUATION (FOR EXAMPLE: AGREEMENT OR DISAGREEMENT) MAY BE INDICATED IN THE SPACE PROVIDED BELOW.

I have reviewed this document and discussed the contents with my manager. My signature means that I have been advised of my performance status and does not necessarily imply that I agree with this evaluation.	Employee's Signature	Date

MANAGEMENT REVIEW

OPTIONAL COMMENTS:

Reviewer's Signature	Print Name	Date

NBD 6531 6/76

Figure 7-1.   Performance appraisal form (page 3).

128

areas of responsibility of the person being evaluated. Standards should be quantified and reasonable, but should require some effort. Objectives should represent strides for improvement of performance, not merely aim at maintaining the status quo. Typically, six to ten well-chosen objectives will be appropriate for defining comprehensive job objectives. The "Responsibilities" column is used for key words describing the responsibility, and the objective itself is stated in the adjacent column. Figure 7-2 is an illustration of some possible objectives for a shift manager in the computer services group. The same responsibility is listed twice in each case, with both an appropriate and an inappropriate objective shown. The difference is clear. The correct objectives establish specific targets of performance that can be measured.

Some managers and subordinates who are new to this system will state unequivocally that the objectives for their positions cannot be quantified. Be persistent, because a little imagination will find answers for virtually any job. The objective-setting process should be a joint process between employee and supervisor. This ensures that the employee is committed to the objectives. Ultimately, the superior must prevail if someone tries to intentionally set low standards, although this is normally not the case. Very often the employee will suggest higher standards than the superior.

The "Changes in Performance Plan" section is used to change the plan when external factors beyond the control of the employee occur. These may be changes to objectives or additional objectives. The "Optional Additional Plans" section is intended for the top performers. It is the extra-credit concept of the old school days. These objectives are targets of achievement beyond the scope of the normal responsibility of the position. Overall evaluations are raised by accomplishment of these objectives, but they are disregarded in evaluation if not achieved.

Evaluating Performance

The second page of the performance appraisal form is for the actual evaluation. This page is completed by the manager. Actual achievements are recorded, and a numeric rating is assigned to each according to the definitions at the top right. Generally, "competent"

PERFORMANCE PLANNING	
RESPONSIBILITIES (KEY WORDS TO DESCRIBE THE MAJOR ELEMENTS OF THIS EMPLOYEE'S JOB)	PERFORMANCE FACTORS AND/OR RESULTS TO BE ACHIEVED (A MORE SPECIFIC STATEMENT OF EMPLOYEE'S KEY RESPONSIBILITIES/GOALS EMPLOYEE CAN REASONABLY BE EXPECTED TO ACHIEVE IN COMING PERIOD.)
Costs (Correct)	Maintain costs within the approved budget plan with a tolerable 10% variance
Costs (Incorrect)	Minimize cost expenditures
Service (Correct)	Reduce late outputs from current level of 3.6% to 2.5% of deliveries
Service (Incorrect)	Improve timely deliveries of work
Hardware Utilization (Correct)	Reduce rerun time from 2% of production time to 1%
Hardware Utilization (Incorrect)	Cut reruns
Employee Relations (Correct)	Reduce shift turnover from 24% annually to 15%
Employee Relations (Incorrect)	Improve morale
CHANGES IN PERFORMANCE PLAN (MAY BE RECORDED ANYTIME DURING THE APPRAISAL PERIOD.)	
OPTIONAL ADDITIONAL PLANS (WHERE CONSIDERED APPROPRIATE BY MANAGER AND EMPLOYEE.)	

Figure 7-2. Sample performance objectives.

130

ratings are for objectives that are satisfactorily achieved; the other ratings are for objectives excelled or not achieved, as appropriate. The two boxes on the lower right-hand side are used only as needed. For example, punctuality would never be a part of the objectives for a professional, but if there was a serious problem in this area, it is noted under "Continuing Responsibilities." Likewise, it is assumed that professionals will work with their peers. If there is a major problem or the person is a valuable informal leader, this can be noted under "Relationships with Others." When all evaluations are completed, the overall rating is noted in the appropriate box. This rating should not be a mere arithmetic mean, because not all objectives have equal value. A judgment must be made after carefully considering all factors.

Naturally, if the performance appraisal system is to be useful in improving performance, the results of the evaluations need to be reviewed with the person evaluated. The last page provides a form for this session. The counseling summary is completed by the manager prior to the review. He lists the strengths and weaknesses of the employee which he feels significantly affected the overall evaluation. This information is for the benefit of the employee. The next two sections are for comments by the manager and the employee after the review session. A second-level management review can be useful, and a space is provided for this purpose too.

It will take some experience with the system before everyone will feel comfortable with it. Managers and employees find in the long run that it is the fairest approach and soon come to regard it highly. Because of the vital nature of the process, assistance from outside the EDP department might be quite useful. An in-house personnel manager or an outside consultant can be a worthwhile aid when installing a new system.

Predicting Promotability

The results-oriented manager maintains that the evaluation of skills and characteristics is subjective, subject to error, and useless for the purposes of performance evaluation. This is a true statement. On the other hand, relying only on the objective appraisal evaluations can promote elevating people to their level of incompetence. The results-oriented approach tells whether or not an individual has

131

performed to standards in his current position, but it does not necessarily predict his performance in a higher-level position, because the skills required will differ, at least in degree, as levels change. If an individual is promoted as long as he receives good performance evaluations, all but a very few will eventually reach their level of incompetence.

This dilemma dictates the need for another type of personnel evaluation. This is an additional requirement, not intended to replace the earlier methodology. On an annual basis, each employee is evaluated in terms of his promotability. The promotability evaluation is done at a time totally separate from the performance evaluation and neither is affected by nor affects the performance evaluation.

The process of evaluating promotability involves defining the normal career path for each employee. Then the skills required for the likely position of promotion are identified, and the employee's abilities in this area are evaluated. Sometimes, unfavorable ratings are merely a matter of a lack of training and experience. In that case, a personal development plan should be designed. In other cases, it will be determined that the individual does not have the ability to progress. Then the employee should be told this, regardless of how painful it might be to everyone. Keep in mind that even a person who has a very high performance rating may have peaked out. For example, some of the best programmers would be terrible project managers.

This approach may be criticized as self-defeating, and some would cite examples as the one above, about the skilled programmer. The manager may well cause the employee to seek other employment, the critics say, by telling him he is not promotable. This is quite possible, but it is not sensible to let the employee proceed with unrealistic expectations, and sooner or later, he will figure out the situation anyway. So keeping the evaluation a secret only prolongs the inevitable. When approached properly, the employee might be able to see his weaknesses and adjust his own expectations. One cautionary measure, though, is not to run to the employee the minute a conclusion is reached, since this is a subjective evaluation and there is room for error. Something of such importance to employer and employee should be given serious deliberation.

-8-

Managing Hardware Resources

MANAGING the computer hardware resource is less difficult than managing personnel, because there are fewer variables and no emotional issues to deal with. It should be remembered that there are many technical considerations relevant to the management of sophisticated computer equipment. These are beyond the scope of this book. The issues considered here are those of direct concern to management, such as vendor selection, configuration selection, utilization objectives, reliability, performance analysis, and capacity planning.

VENDOR SELECTION

Vendor selection is not the simple process it once was, merely because of the number of vendors now in the marketplace. Not only are there many unique vendors, but there are dozens more specializing in plug-compatible everything in the market. The process of selecting vendors is simpler for the established EDP department, because software compatibility problems normally restrict the department to its mainframe vendor after it has a significant investment in software. The company choosing its first computer can be virtually bewildered by the choices it faces.

This discussion assumes that the selection is being made by a

133

company that will use its computers principally for general business applications. It is also assumed that EDP management and top management have established quality service as the first priority of the EDP department. This environment requires a general-purpose computer. The vendor must offer a broad range of computer models so that the company can start small and upgrade as it grows. The vendor should also have a full complement of peripheral devices and terminals. Even if they are not needed now, the devices may be needed in the future. Keep in mind that the initial selection can be a long-range commitment. The vendor must provide a complement of system software, technical support and an established field maintenance service.

Once the potential vendors have been identified, each should be notified that a proposal for a computer configuration is desired. The request is generally referred to as a request for proposal (RFP). The RFP contains a brief description of the activities of the company and of the applications planned for the computer and gives as much data on anticipated volumes as possible. Remember, the more detail vendors are given, the better the quality of their proposals can be, so spend some time on the RFP. If there are any predetermined requirements, such as the capability for terminal processing, note these in the RFP.

One pitfall to avoid in competitive bidding is allowing the effort to become an auction. There are some vendors in the industry who will present a proposal for one price and then begin slashing prices if they feel they are losing the business. When more than one vendor using this practice is involved, chaos can develop. From a business standpoint, these vendors either overpriced their original proposals or are subsequently cutting prices to a point that doesn't make sense. In the latter case, they may try to convince a company that they are willing to offer low prices because the company is considered a "prestige customer." Don't be fooled by this; no vendor is in the business for any reason other than to make a profit, and sooner or later, they will find a way to get more money. The fact that this is a long-range commitment cannot be stressed enough. A deadline should be set for proposals, and the proposals should be submitted in writing and must include a specific configuration and a firm price. Let vendors know in advance that the price is final and don't let them sell general concepts with a promise of a proposal to follow later.

Evaluating Vendor Responses

After proposals are received, they must be analyzed and a vendor chosen. Price, although not necessarily the most important criterion, is a good place to start. Guard against the "lowball" price. Some vendors will intentionally propose a smaller configuration than required to keep the price down. After the configuration is installed and bottlenecks are found, they admit that they and the customer "jointly" erred in estimating capacity needs and propose an upgrade at a higher cost. Evaluate the relative computing power of the various proposals and be suspicious of one which is clearly smaller. If there is no in-house expertise on the relative processing power of configurations, get some outside opinions, as vendor claims will not always be totally accurate.

Make sure that prices compare "apples to apples." Find out what taxes are or aren't included, and if the customer is liable for any taxes. Determine what insurance coverage is included and if maintenance is a part of the contract. Maintenance is often sold in contracts to cover one-, two-, or three-shift maintenance and priced accordingly, so the exact terms of the maintenance agreement must be known. Some vendors pass along benefits of investment tax credit provisions to the customer. Determine each vendor's policy and consult with company tax counselors to verify the benefit to the company.

After evaluation of the economic side comes an evaluation of the configuration itself. The processing power of the configuration is, of course, crucial. Make sure the configuration selected meets the company's needs. The performance of peripheral devices is quite important. Inadequate tapes, disks, and printers will slow down the whole machine. Ensure that device types are compatible with needs. Determine how many additional peripherals of each type can be added without upgrading the central processors. And, by all means, find out how much the processor capacity can be upgraded without having to convert user-developed software. Claims of upward compatibility of software are often exaggerated, so get some outside information.

The systems software provided by the vendor is also vitally important. Understand the user responsibility and how much manpower is required to maintain the systems software. Know the functions it provides and the complexity of use for operators, application programmers, and systems programmers. Reliability of systems software is critical to the reliability of the entire configuration.

Overall reliability of the configuration is the next area of consideration. The reputation of the field maintenance group for each vendor in the company's area should be evaluated. Get as many statistics as possible in respect to reliability. The duration of failures is as good a measurement of maintenance quality, and as important, as the number of failures.

Vendor support in terms of technical assistance is another factor. Some vendors commit more resources and have more customer programs than others. Itemize the services provided by each and compare these services with the installation needs. Related considerations are the number of experienced professionals in the market who are familiar with each vendor's technology. When packaged software is to be used by the installation, the number of software houses providing the type of packages desired is important. Market opportunities for plug-compatible peripherals and terminals offer future advantages.

After careful consideration of the preceding points, the vendor is selected. There are some methods available which use evaluation indexes and weighted averages to make the final selection, but these are of marginal value. The ratings are still subjective. Very few individuals are qualified to evaluate hardware technology from an engineering standpoint, so keep the consideration on a business level. Basically, the best computer is the one which serves the installation requirements, provides the most computing power for the money, has the best long-range potential, and meets service and support requirements.

USING MORE THAN ONE VENDOR

The new installation should order the entire initial configuration from one vendor. The implementation problems will be numerous enough without complicating the situation with multiple vendors. But later, when they are established, EDP departments should consider the options for plug-compatible hardware and software to determine potential cost savings.

There are numerous companies in the business of providing all types of products to be used with some large manufacturers' equipment. The products are normally presented as better than the vendor's own at reduced prices. The statement may be true in a few cases, but normally the advantage of the plug-compatibles is price. In evaluating proposals for plug-compatibles, all the financial considerations, such as maintenance costs, taxes, and insurance, must be considered.

EDP managers should be cautious of non-mainframe vendors' systems software. Some good teleprocessing monitors and data base management systems are on the market today, but application programs are highly dependent on their design, which may be different from the vendor's own. This situation creates a very risky environment in terms of future compatibility as architecture changes. Certain special-purpose utility software packages can be very beneficial, but systems software should come from the main frame vendor.

Evaluating vendors of plug-compatible hardware is much like the original evaluation of computer vendors. The point which needs extra investigations is field maintenance, as many of the smaller vendors do not have field support in all geographic areas. Because some of these vendors are relatively unknown compared to the large mainframe vendors, a study of the company itself is often needed. A financial analysis and general business review can be useful. An EDP manager doesn't want equipment with no one to service it as a result of the vendor going out of business.

A strategy for plug-compatible hardware should be established before jumping into the market. Many companies have created problems for themselves by installing a central processor from one vendor, a few peripherals from another, a few more from another, and so on. This creates a ''fruit cocktail'' type of environment, which can evolve into a maintenance nightmare. A definite negative of mixed shops is the finger-pointing between vendors of various components of the configuration when maintenance problems occur.

Coordinating various vendors is a time-consuming activity with a cost.

Of all vendors offering the plug-compatibles, some are quite excellent, and some are not. Investigate all the principal vendors for a given product before deciding, rather than sign up with the first salesman offering attractive cost savings. The best strategy is to find a vendor with an established reputation and get a proposal for a large piece of the installation, such as all the tape drives if there are many of them. In this way, you might realize substantial savings while limiting vendors to two or three. When the business is split up helter-skelter, there is a mess, and the EDP department spreads the business so much, it winds up not being a very important customer of anybody.

Software-Compatible Processors

The area of software-compatible central processors deserves a few special comments. Previously, it was noted that once the central processor is chosen, the installation is essentially locked in because of software compatibility. This is true with the main vendors of computer systems. However, vendors of software-compatible central processors change this by offering processors compatible with another vendor's software. These vendors produce central processors designed to replace another vendor's computer. They do not sell complete sytems but only the computers themselves, which are guaranteed to be compatible with the software of the machine being replaced.

This is a relatively new phenomonen, so it would be a little premature to evaluate this option. Some of these vendors show promise of quality products with lower prices. The final judgment must wait, though, until these vendors prove themselves able to support a large installed base in the field, and until the inevitable reaction of the vendors whose market share is threatened by software-compatible processors is determined and assessed.

THE FINAL CONFIGURATION

Picking the exact configuration for any installation is difficult. There are no precise formulas for determining memory size, number of peripherals, peripherals speeds, and the like. The process is further complicated by the fact that there are so many options available from the vendor. The customer can, in essence, customize his system to fit his need. The process is relatively easier for the established EDP department. Management looks at the current utilization and compares it to standards. When an upgrade is required, management compares the current computer to larger alternatives and selects the appropriate model. For first-time users, the choice is not as clear-cut. They have a shopping list of applications, but probably haven't designed any of them yet. No one really knows for sure how much of a given computer each application will require. Experience of EDP personnel with the applications contemplated and knowledge of the vendor's models must be used as the basis of the estimate. The vendor should be expected to help in this area. However, be prepared to make changes later. Keep financial arrangements flexible; don't buy or sign a long-term lease on the first computer.

MAINTAINING RELIABILITY

Maintaining hardware reliability is vital to the EDP department and an important management activity. If the department has a large equipment investment, it has a right to demand on-site maintenance service from the vendor. Smaller shops will have to rely on a central dispatcher. In either case, EDP management should have a clear understanding with the vendor in terms of how quickly responses should be expected when problems are reported. Also, an understanding should be reached as to when vendor specialists should be called and other escalation measures should be undertaken because immediate resolution of a problem did not occur. No set of rules will apply to every situation, but guidelines can be developed which are useful in measuring service. EDP managers must use reasonable business sense; however, vendor problems with staffing or whatever can be given only a limited amount of sympathy.

Most major vendors claim to have comprehensive preventive maintenance programs. In ongoing practice these never seem to be carried out. Preventive maintenance really will make a difference in hardware performance, especially in respect to mechanical devices like printers and card readers. Get the vendor to commit to a regular preventive maintenance schedule and then follow up on him to ensure it is regularly completed.

The final and crucial analysis is how well the hardware actually runs. The vendor probably won't like to commit himself to standards, but he will agree to it if his arm is twisted a little. Establish standards that measure both the number of occurrences and the total downtime. Regular reporting against the standards will communicate to everyone the status of the hardware.

UTILIZATION STANDARDS

Naturally, everyone wants to get the most out of computer equipment. The higher the utilization, the lower the cost per job processed. The capacity of equipment in terms of the compute cycles per second and similar measures is readily available from technical manuals. But these do not represent the real capacity of the equipment. Scheduling methodology attempts to minimize peaks in computer work load; however, these peaks can never be refined so that the computer work load is a straight-line chart. Therefore, utilization must be evaluated in great detail over a long period of time. A computer that has 30 percent average utilization might not have the capacity to handle mandatory peak periods. Therefore, assuming work cannot be shifted, the capacity of this computer has been exceeded for the installation.

The important point for management is to be cautious about statistical summaries showing average utilization and to avoid drawing erroneous conclusions. Some EDP managers have fallen into this trap and reduced equipment, and then were amazed that work did not get completed on schedule. However, EDP management must set some objectives for overall utilization to achieve economy. Each installation must determine that level itself.

Utilization Measurement
Measuring utilization of hardware and interpreting the data is a fairly technical activity. This should be the responsibility of the

technical development group. In the larger EDP departments, performance measurement is a function of the hardware planning section. Besides hardware measurement, this group is responsible for the overall throughput performance of the hardware. Today's complex environment requires sophisticated tools to measure utilization accurately. Many excellent software and hardware monitors are on the market for this purpose, and the in-house systems programmer will be more than eager to discuss them.

Hardware measurement and performance tuning is a highly technical subject. EDP managers need not worry about all the detail, but they should understand that an aggressive program of this type can make substantial differences in how much work is obtained from a given configuration. Channel configuration, disk data-set allocation, and many similar areas can have a major impact. The investments here can pay big dividends. The technical support personnel should identify improvements in the physical configuration, in regard to software tuning, and also in scheduling and general operating procedures that will increase throughput.

Capacity Planning

Besides maximizing the capacity of the configuration, the performance measurement activity should identify trends and future changes in the configuration. This requires development of long-range capacity planning techniques, which are necessary for many reasons. Hardware upgrades and changes in supporting facilities cannot be made on a day's notice. And the installation cannot afford to wait until a new application bogs down processing to realize it has run out of capacity. So, the EDP department must attempt to plan requirements as far in advance as possible.

Unfortunately, hardware planning is still more of an art that a science. There are a few simulation programs for predicting the utilization requirements of a given software design, and there should be many more tools like this in the future. However, these tools are limited and have a certain margin of error, and sometimes capacity planning will require estimates before systems are even designed.

Despite these drawbacks, a reasonable analysis is better than no plan at all. Estimates can be made for planned applications on the basis of simulations and in-house experience. Where possible, new applications should be compared with current ones in terms of size. Growth patterns can then be identified and added to current workload figures to identify probable timing of upgrades.

Until capacity planning is further refined, the established EDP department must be cautious if growth is continuous and fast-paced. Like the first-time computer users, EDP managers in these environments should keep their options open in respect to long-term financial commitments. Many hardware purchases that looked like a good deal compared to rental rates have gone sour because the computer was outgrown sooner then expected.

COMPUTER USE PRICING

A final issue in respect to hardware management is the pricing of computer usage. The pricing is important to feasibility studies for new applications and allocating costs. Some users will tend to look at computer time as "free" once a computer is installed. This is most often the case in installations where the computer equipment is purchased or acquired on a long-term lease with no extra usage charges. The logic goes that as long as the computer is paid for and there is capacity, there is no incremental cost of increasing the utilization. This is a nice argument for a user trying to justify a marginal application, but it can have extremely harmful effects. The short run may prove the argument true. Assuming the proposed job is a one-time affair, costing could be done in an incremental way. However, in the long run, every job contributes to the growth of the computer requirements and hence must pay its own way. Otherwise, theoretically a lot of "free" applications could lead to the need to upgrade computers, with an expenditure that is not cost-justifiable.

This concludes the chapter on hardware management as well as the general discussion of organization and other techniques of EDP management. Chapter 9 will cover the development of the EDP plan.

–9–

EDP Planning

PLANNING is the management function most talked about and least carried out. All managers talk of their planning responsibilities, but many have no idea how to go about planning in either a long-range or a short-range mode. This is not a weakness peculiar to EDP managers. Managers in many company functions, including some top managers, have no grasp of planning techniques. A chief executive officer of a major corporation once presented a handful of objectives as the corporation's long-range plan. Other managers have organized random ideas into a priority of programs and called them the plan.

Planning is hard work. It requires a methodology, thoughtful analysis, and attention to detail. A real plan identifies the targets to be achieved, what must be done to achieve them, who will complete the required steps, when they will be completed, and how much they will cost.

THE NEED FOR PLANNING

Planning is fundamental to the EDP department or any other function. The plan provides direction of effort, coordination of activities, and a prescribed manner to accomplish objectives. It gives order to the function and offers a basis for evaluating progress.

An EDP department without a plan is characterized by reoccurring crises, conflicting or duplicated activities, and a mode of reacting to various factors as opposed to progressing uniformly toward a stated goal. The plan provides logic to the sequence of activities and establishes priorities for EDP resources. EDP resources are utilized more efficiently in a planned environment, too.

All these benefits will lead to an EDP organization more responsive to the business needs and user service requirements. Given these considerations, there can be no justification for any EDP manager not to aggressively carry out the planning activities.

STAGES OF PLANNING

To develop effective EDP plans, three stages of planning are required. These are the long-range business plan of the company, the long-range EDP plan, and the operating EDP plan. The business plan defines the objectives and programs of the business and is the basis for the long-range EDP plan. The long-range EDP plan determines the basic strategy and major programs of the EDP department for a five-year period and is the basis of the operating plan. The operating plan provides a one-year set of objectives and detailed projects, resources, and budgets.

The long-range and operating plans differ in more ways than merely their term. First, because of its longer term, the long-range plan will be more general because of a greater number of unknowns. The long-range plan will be less specific in terms of how programs will be completed and who will complete them. Plan cost estimates are rougher in the long-range plan and will often be in terms of ranges rather than definitive as in the operating plan. The long-range plan states the overall definition of what is to be done and the general approach. The operating plans are concerned with detailed steps for achieving certain parts of the long-range plan. Therefore, the long-range EDP plan will be prepared at the department level and will not address in detail subordinate organizational divisions, whereas the operating plan must encompass each element of the organization.

No activity can be left out in respect to the three phases of planning. Without a business plan, the EDP plan can only be based on EDP management's guesses of the business direction or, worse, be developed without regard to the business direction. An operating plan without benefit of the insight of a long-range EDP plan leads to commitments to activities that may not be consistent with one another in the long run. The long-range plan provides overall targets for the department to pace itself toward, ensures that all the pieces fit together, and provides a basis for long-term decisions such as lease versus purchase of hardware.

THE BASIC PLANNING PROCESS

The planning process has five basic steps. These steps are necessary for any type of planning, either long-range or short-range. The following list outlines the five elements of the planning process. The definitions are somewhat general in nature and need some further explanation for practical application.

Step	Result
Determine goals.	Establishes where the organization is to go.
Complete the situation analysis.	Summarizes where the organization is.
Set objectives.	Defines in more detail where the organization wants to be.
Establish programs.	Tells how the organization is to get there.
Project costs.	Presents the costs of programs.

Chapter 1 defined a goal for EDP as follows: to provide cost-effective EDP services of a high quality while providing for future needs and minimizing operating costs. This goal is a statement of the guiding philosophy. It tells where the organization wants to go. The goal is intentionally not quantified, because the assumption is that there is no limit to what can be achieved. The goal generally changes only as a result of a basic change in the business. The value of the goal is to set the stage for the subsequent steps in the planning process by defining the priority of efforts. The above goal clearly tells what areas should be emphasized by EDP department management.

Before any specific plans can be completed, the organization must undertake a situation analysis. The end product of this is an analysis of the department in relation to its goal and a set of conclusions to be used for planning purposes. The scope of the situation analysis must be broad enough to provide an understanding of the environment to the extent necessary for developing a comprehensive plan.

A good starting point for the situation analysis is a review of the prior plan's objectives. Achievements and failures are noted and variations explained. The status of planned projects and the budget from the previous plan are likewise analyzed. After the review of the most recent past, an evaluation of the current operation follows. Problems and opportunities are listed and analyzed. Problem definition requires careful analysis. It deals with results-oriented issues, such as service problems and cost control, and more specific problems, such as control methods that seem to be failing, hardware problems, and similar items. The other side is an analysis of opportunities that have arisen. Hardware throughput greater than expected or a lower employee turnover rate than historically incurred are relevant examples.

External factors are the next group that should be covered in the situation analysis. These are factors outside the EDP department which can affect its performance. Changes in company hiring and salary policies could be important. Profit results and cost-cutting programs of the company are other examples. External factors also include circumstances outside the company. Vendor performance and policies could greatly influence the EDP plan. Government regulations are significant in some industries. Established requirements, such as those contained in the prior plans or others defined by management, should be noted in the situation analysis. Requests for changes in service from the users are documented here when they are not reported as problems with EDP service.

After all these areas are analyzed, the situation analysis is completed with a summary of conclusions. The conclusions net out the status of the function at the time and the areas of special emphasis for the future period. These conclusions are the basis for determining the objectives of the EDP department.

Objectives were discussed in relation to the performance appraisal system in Chapter 7. The same types of objectives are used for the planning process. Objectives are specific, quantified statements, tied to the basic goal, that tell where the organization desires to be at the end of the planning period. The objectives define in which specific areas resources will be utilized.

The determination of objectives is based on the situation analysis. Objectives for each planning unit should comprise eight to ten statements of what is to be achieved for the planning period. Objectives should cover all the major responsibilities of the function and emphasize the areas highlighted in the situation analysis. Unlike the goal, objectives will change with each planning period. A useful format is to begin each statement with an action word such as complete, reduce, or maintain. The statement is then completed quantifying the target. The statements should be relatively brief.

The objectives in the plan tie closely to the objectives defined in the performance appraisal system. In fact, the performance objectives of the manager of an organizational unit will be very close to the objectives for the unit as defined in the planning process. Performance objectives for subordinates are also based on the objectives in the plan, but are more specific and tailored to the individual's specific responsibilities.

Once objectives are set, programs or projects must be established to achieve them and cost estimates must be prepared. Given that objectives are targets of performance, it is a foregone conclusion that at least one project is required to meet each objective. The first four steps essentially define the plan of action. The last step is to determine the cost. Ideally, the cost of each program as well as the total departmental costs are determined.

LONG-RANGE PLANNING

Long-range planning, although following the five basic steps outlined in the preceding section, has special requirements. Again, the first step in this process is a review of the EDP goal and the long-range business plan. As previously stated, the director of data processing should be the moving force in the planning process. This is not to indicate that many other key staff members should not participate—and methods to encourage broad participation will be discussed later—but the director must organize and direct the over-all activity. The first step he must take is to complete the situation analysis. This effort should not be rushed, because a penetrating analysis is important to the success of the overall plan.

On the basis of the requirements of the overall business plan and the situation analysis just completed, the director establishes objectives for the department for the five-year period. This phase of planning must accomplish two things: (1) establish the five-year objectives and (2) translate these five-year objectives into specific objectives for each year within the plan. In other words, steps toward achievement are defined, allowing progress to be monitored at shorter intervals and providing a basis for objectives in the operating plans of each year. Table 9-1 is a sample format of how the long-range-plan objectives can be presented. The table shows progress for each year toward the stated objectives.

After the objectives are documented, programs for the five-year period must be developed. In a general sense there are two types of programs which are included in the long-range plan. The first are those projects directly aimed at supporting the objectives. These are the projects that dictate how EDP will do its business. These projects will represent activities such as the development of new methodologies, organization structure changes, and personnel programs. For example, Table 9-1 lists an objective to reduce outside recruiting to 50 percent of new positions. This requires a program, if not already in place, to establish career path and training programs to develop in-house talent for these positions. Also, programs relating to technical strategies may be required. Again referring to Table 9-1, the objective to limit cost increases to 5 percent per year may require cost improvement programs just to offset inflation. Programs such as improving resource utilization or installing a hardware system with improved price/performance ratio may be relevant. The objective to install data base technology may require several software, hardware, and related projects.

148

Table 9-1. Long-range EDP objectives.

DESCRIPTION	FIVE-YEAR TARGET	SPECIFIC ANNUAL TARGETS				
		1979	1980	1981	1982	1983
Limit cost increases to an overall of 25% of total budget.	25%	5%	5%	5%	5%	5%
Complete 100% of projects within plan.	100%	30%	30%	15%	15%	10%
Reduce late deliveries of reports from 3.6% to .5%.	.5%	3%	2.0%	1.5%	1.0%	.5%
Reduce teleprocessing downtime from 1.5% to .5%.	.5%	1.3%	1.1%	.9%	.7%	.5%
Reduce outside recruiting from 100% of new positions to 50%.	50%	95%	90%	80%	70%	50%
Complete implementation of data base environment through 100% conversion of application systems.	100%	5%	15%	40%	70%	100%

The other group of projects comprises those relating directly to products and services to be provided by the EDP department. They define what EDP will do.

From a logical standpoint, the application plan is the basis of this portion of the EDP plan. Realistically, no EDP plan can cover a longer period than the application plan. The business plan of the company probably defines new application requirements resulting from the company's plan to provide new products, its desire to improve the performance of certain application functions, or management's desire for more types of information. User departments will directly supply application requests, some of which may have resulted from previous recommendations to them by the EDP department.

The next step in the development of the application plan is to sort the projects into a recommended sequence of priorities. The priorities should reflect the parameters of the business plan, expressed desires of the users, and an evaluation of any dependent projects within the group of application systems. Then the rather difficult task of estimating is undertaken. Most of the application projects probably have had little more review than a preliminary analysis at this point, so estimates will not be too precise. However, some cost basis is needed for evaluating the plan. Perhaps estimating with ranges of cost is the most practical approach. The members of the systems development group who are most familiar with the proposed applications should perform the estimating.

As discussed in relation to project control methodology, the plan for a given work load is a function of the time allowed for the completion and the resources available. As either the time or the resources change, the other is affected. For example, if the application group requires 50 man-years for work that is to be completed in five years, then ten people are required. If the policy were to limit the staff to five people, then the projects would take ten years. There are of course many variations. The business plan, the subsequent EDP situation analysis, and long-range EDP objectives will determine the guidelines. On the basis of these, a determination is made as to which projects will be included in the current five-year plan. Actual costs are determined by applying wage rates to the number of people.

After the application plan, the hardware plan, the systems software plan, the facility plan, and the staff plan are developed, in that order. From a practical standpoint each of these is a part of different EDP groups' activities. The long-range plan is concerned more with this order than with individual group plans; therefore, the emphasis should be on coordinating the logical development of the EDP plan, not on individual plans of EDP groups. Formalizing group objectives contributes little to the long-range EDP plan.

Using the projected impact of the application plan as a basis, the hardware plan should document the anticipated changes in the configuration, followed by a definition of projects required to implement the changes. Similarly, the systems software changes required to support the hardware changes are defined, and these, too, are translated into implementation projects. The systems software project list can include systems software projects not relating directly to hardware changes. These may include projects to provide software to meet new application design requirements or even other studies, such as interactive programming support and general utilities. Facility plans continue in the same vein, listing changes and defining implementation projects.

The hardware systems, software, and facility projects, as well as the projects relating directly to the support of EDP objectives, are sorted according to the resources that will be used for their completion. The projects within each category are prioritized, giving special attention to the interrelationships between projects. Time and cost estimates are completed for these projects too. Priorities are established to determine which of the projects will be completed within the current five-year plan, although those projects that directly support an application requirement cannot easily be dropped.

When all projects have been inventoried and development manpower has been estimated, more detailed scheduling must be completed. The projects for the entire five-year period are known, as well as the time estimates for each. Now specific schedules in terms of start and stop dates for each project must be developed. Dates will be a reflection of the priority of the project and its overall scope. It is extremely important at this point to carefully analyze the interrelationships among projects again. Projects required for the completion of others must be undertaken first. A Gantt chart or similar technique is virtually mandatory for this activity.

Once the schedules for all projects are complete, the final step in the construction of the long-range plan is the budget estimate. For future comparison, the budget should be broken down by year, as suggested for the objectives and shown in Table 9-2. The minimum requirement for the budget is the development of direct costs associated with carrying out the programs defined and maintaining ongoing production. Other costs such as for supplies, floor space, and lighting are preferable, but optional. Their inclusion depends on whether company management desires to use the projections for financial planning or merely intends to use them as a means of evaluating proposed EDP activities.

The budget for development projects has already been determined

Table 9-2. Long-range-plan budget.

COST ITEM	FIVE-YEAR TOTAL	COSTS BY YEAR				
		1979	1980	1981	1982	1983
Management and Administration	1,930,000	320,000	350,000	380,000	420,000	460,000
Development						
Application systems	3,775,000	650,000	700,000	800,000	800,000	825,000
Technical enhancements	600,000	100,000	110,000	120,000	130,000	140,000
EDP management projects	350,000	60,000	65,000	70,000	75,000	80,000
Total	4,725,000	810,000	875,000	990,000	1,005,000	1,045,000
Maintenance						
Application systems	1,340,000	200,000	230,000	265,000	300,000	345,000
Systems software	259,000	30,000	33,000	36,000	80,000	80,000
Total	1,599,000	230,000	263,000	301,000	380,000	425,000
Operations						
Staff	2,900,000	450,000	500,000	600,000	650,000	700,000
Hardware	6,000,000	1,000,000	1,000,000	1,200,000	1,200,000	1,600,000
Other equipment and supplies	600,000	100,000	110,000	120,000	130,000	140,000
Total	9,500,000	1,550,000	1,610,000	1,920,000	1,980,000	2,440,000
Overhead						
Floor space, lighting, etc.	840,000	150,000	150,000	180,000	180,000	180,000
Contingency	1,800,000	300,000	300,000	400,000	400,000	400,000
Grand Total	20,394,000	3,360,000	3,548,000	4,171,000	4,365,000	4,950,000

as a function of the estimating process. Estimates for management and administrative positions must be made. A maintenance budget for current applications and systems software must be determined as well as costs for any purchased software or outside consultants. The annual hardware expenditure anticipated is extracted from the hardware plan. Systems software development costs must be determined also. Staff levels for the computer services group are determined according to work loads. And the cost of operating supplies and other overhead items are estimated.

The cost categories or line items in Table 9-2 are fairly obvious. The figures for each category summarize cost by major activity—development, maintenance, and operations. Another presentation of costs by cost type that may be desirable would be similar to the one in Table 9-2, except that the line items would be total staff, total hardware, and so on, as opposed to sorting costs by how the resources are used.

Note a "Contingency" category in Table 9-2. To be realistic, the budget must provide for unplanned activities. The further the point from the date of the plan, the more likely such activities are, and the higher the contingency allowance should be.

A recap of the end products of the long-range plan will serve as a good review of the process. The situation analysis is first in the order of presentation. Next are the objectives. The overall chart of projects and schedules should be third. If more detail of projects is desirable, a recap of projects by category, giving a brief description of each and start and stop dates, is useful. Finally, the budget exhibits follow. The plan need not be gold-embossed, but neat binding certainly adds to its professionalism.

A couple of cautionary notes are warranted. The programs in the plan are generally included on the basis of only preliminary review and subjective judgment. Therefore, each project is still subject to further feasibility studies and justification. Management's approval of the plan does not automatically approve each program. On the other hand, the dates and budgets were developed by EDP management using this same preliminary information. So, EDP management cannot be held accountable for all variations, although it should be required to explain obviously absurd projections.

The long-range plan requires the approval of executive management before it is implemented. The smart EDP director will review major portions along the way to minimize the potential of rework. However, a final review is required. Qualitative as well as quantitative aspects of objectives, project inventories and priorities, and budgets are all part of the executive review. Final judgment on whether the plan satisfactorily meets the business needs is also the executive prerogative.

One word of common sense about long-range planning is necessary. If the EDP department is fraught with service problems, don't insist on spending a lot of time on long-range planning before addressing those current problems. This is the "quick fix" strategy presented as a part of problem control. Long-range planning is not the right priority, nor will it be fruitful in an environment where basic requirements are not being met. A short-term plan is required to establish control before a full-range program is undertaken.

THE OPERATING PLAN

Operating planning follows the same general process as long-range planning but has its own unique requirements. The foundation of the operating plan is of course the long-range EDP plan. The operating plan is much more specific in regard to the steps for completing programs, and much more precise in its estimates. The operating plan is the level for which EDP management becomes really accountable.

The director of data processing begins this process again with a situation analysis of the forthcoming year. Objectives are set for the current year for the EDP department, consistent with the objectives established by the long-range plan, although certain additional objectives may be desirable. Basically, the director defines what is to be achieved for the current year in order to achieve the objectives of the long-range plan. Projects and programs for the year are initially extracted from the long-range plan. Also, additional projects may be defined which were not in the original projection. The situation analysis, the objectives, and the projects are documented and given to group managers. Projects defined by the director of EDP are assigned to appropriate groups.

The group managers repeat this process and present the results to section and shift managers, respectively, who do the same. This part—determining objectives and programs—is the "top down" aspect of the planning process. The remainder of the process is essentially a "bottom up" technique. Section and shift managers define how and by whom each program will be completed and develop plans as they relate to their own sphere of responsibility. The plans are then summarized upward by organizational level until the EDP department plan is complete.

The flow of planning is an often discussed problem. Arguments about top-down and bottom-up are frequent. But the effective plan is really the result of an interactive process. Top management defines its desires, and subordinate levels add additional programs and define how to achieve the whole plan. In the real environment there must be some joint discussion at each stage.

Once the section manager completes his situation analysis and objectives, he completes the project inventory for his own section. Again, for each objective there should be a specific project or projects to demonstrate how the objective will be met. Often no project has yet been defined for an objective. In that case, additional projects must be defined. Other projects that have arisen, not necessarily as a part of the overall strategy, are acceptable too. For example, the technical development group may define a project to evaluate a new technology even if the area is not part of the overall EDP strategy. However, these later projects would normally be the first to be cut if budget limits are exceeded, because preserving the overall strategy is of primary importance.

Regardless of the source, the project inventory is completed. The next step is to prioritize projects. This may sound unnecessary if it is assumed that all projects are to be completed during the current year, but there may be benefit in completing some earlier in the year. The prioritization also is a guideline to cutting if budgets are higher than desired by management. The plan, even when consistent with

155

the long-range plan, may turn out to be more expensive than allowable for the current year.

Remember to consider any dependent steps when prioritizing projects. Projects between groups and sections may also have a high degree of dependency, and the managers must coordinate the relative priorities and dates of these. The end product of the project inventory is a list of all projects in priority sequence. Each project should be given a name for descriptive purposes. Numerically identifying them will help later for referencing and status reporting.

At this point the planning and project control methodologies begin to marry. Ideally, a detailed project plan is completed for each project on the list, and estimates are assigned to tasks to determine the resources required for each project. The sum of resources of all projects then becomes the total resource required to execute the project plans. This may not be practical in some cases, as it could be too disruptive to ongoing project activity to take the time for such detailed planning. The other option is to do a preliminary estimate on each project as a whole. The accuracy will not be as high this way, so it is a trade-off that management must make.

The next process, scheduling projects and resources, involves more detail than described for long-range planning. The objectives, previously developed, should define the priorities of cost control versus getting projects completed on schedule. An assumption is made about either staff levels or deadlines and the other is calculated as a function of the work load. Detailed scheduling of projects finishes this stage.

Project control was presented in an earlier chapter as a systems management technique. This is because project management is the heart of systems management. However, as implied in the discussion of the planning procedures, all EDP groups, including computer services, will normally have some project activity. The project control techniques are just as applicable for the same reasons as required in the systems development group. When planning manpower resources for projects, the contingency factor must again be considered. If project planning was properly executed, a contingency for estimating errors has already been provided. If project control techniques have not been used, a contingency factor should be added to the project plan. Additionally, a general contingency may be desirable for unexpected projects, as there is always a user with the last-second request that may be impossible to delay until the next year's plan.

The next step in the preparation of the operating plan is the preparation of budgets. These will differ from budget projections made for the long-range plan. The budgets are prepared for the lowest organizational unit, and consolidated upward to develop the EDP department budget. This provides operating budgets for each unit within the organization. Unlike budgets for the long-range plan, which are based on areas of activity, the budgets for the operating plan should be very detailed in respect to cost categories. They should be complete—that is, include all direct costs such as personnel and hardware rental, as well as indirect charges for floor space, lighting, and the like, and company overhead allocations such as a pro rata allocation of executive management costs. This provides a full-cost budget, which can be used as a basis for pricing EDP services and can be included in companywide financial planning.

The budget preparation will differ within groups of the EDP department. The systems groups' budgets are largely staff costs for development work. A factor also has to be added for maintenance, and a contingency reserve for unexpected projects is advisable here, too. The budget is completed with miscellaneous items. Computer services budgeting is a little more complex. Schedules for operations need to be developed for the year on the basis of the methodology discussed in Chapter 6. The hardware plan from the long-range plan must be reviewed and updated as necessary in conjunction with the technical support group. The hardware dollars are extracted accordingly. The schedule and hardware plans are the basis for staff projections. Miscellaneous costs are also added.

Now a plan and a budget have been completed for each section of the EDP department. The next step is to consolidate these plans. Section plans are summarized to create a group plan that will support the group's objectives. The summary of all group plans yields the EDP department plan. If during the top-down portion of the planning process the objectives of each subordinate unit reflect the higher objectives, the consolidated plans will support the objectives of the department.

The plan is now ready to become the operating procedure for the EDP department for the year. It is useless if it is merely bound attractively and placed on a bookshelf. The plan should be the basis of all activity in the EDP department and must be constantly reviewed to ensure that adequate progress is being made. Major activities outside the plan should be barred without high-level management approval. Assuming the plan is realistic, every major activity outside the plan eliminates something within it. Major variations during execution of the plan should be quickly identified. Not only must corrective action for specific variances be taken, but possible impacts on other projects and activities should be determined. The objective is to prevent slippages in one area from throwing off a major portion of the plan. Problems must be identified, isolated, and rectified so that progress can continue in line with the plan.

FUTURE PLAN CHANGES

Plan modification considerations must be carefully evaluated. Theoretically, if all the appropriate people were consulted and all relevant issues were considered, there would be no reason to have to alter the plan. But in the real world, there will be changes that can't be handled even by designated contingency reserves. Even problems in executing the plan can eventually require changes. When these situations occur, the plan must be modified. This should be done in such a way as to minimize the impact. Don't redo the whole plan in midstream if it is not absolutely necessary. In any event, the reason for the revision is important. When changes occur that are beyond the control of EDP management, the objectives as well as project plans and budgets are revised, and EDP management is accountable for the new plan only. When the revisions result from errors of execution, it may be desirable to modify the plan to reflect updated estimates, but EDP management is still accountable for the original plan.

PLANNING PROCEDURES

The planning schedule will vary within each company, dependent on its size and its requirements. The annual planning period should coincide with the company fiscal year so that budget projections can be used for overall profit and cash-flow planning purposes. Normally, the planning cycle begins about a year in advance. The long-range plan is developed during the first half of the year, and the succeeding year's operating plan is completed in the last half. Every succeeding year, the remaining years of the long-range plan are updated and an additional year is added.

Before proceeding with the planning effort, a detailed procedure covering the steps to be completed should be established. The larger the organization is, the more important these procedures are. The procedures should cover the long-range planning and operational planning steps. They should define what is to be done and who is responsible, and establish a schedule for the planning process. A forms-oriented procedure is probably most effective. This approach uses a customized form for each step of the process. Forms become useful guidelines for preparing plans and also ensure standard end products to ease consolidation. As with any activity, the participants in the planning process will need to be trained. Don't assume all managers will know how to complete a situation analysis or how to define thoughtful objectives.

The planning activity in EDP must allow maximum participation of personnel. Users, EDP management, key technicians, and even vendor personnel, depending on the relationship, should participate. Plans cannot be developed in a short time, so planning requirements have to be scheduled in detail. It is a good idea to prepare a project plan even for the planning activity. The planning process should begin with an open discussion of current situations and, hopefully, an imaginative analysis. A very effective approach is to have a meeting with the director and all key managers. Ideally, this meeting would take place outside the company offices so that interruptions are minimized. One or two full days should be set aside, and the meeting should be structured in a way to allow the fullest participation of each member.

159

QUALITY IS NOT INEVITABLE

As a closing note, there is a qualitative factor in planning that should be emphasized. There are many managers who regard planning as paperwork that distracts from their jobs. Others may be unenthusiastic for a number of reasons. The director of data processing must present a good argument for planning requirements and insist on complete commitment by everyone involved. If staff planning groups are formed, their members should be among the most talented in the EDP department.

The planning process may well be the single most important activity of the entire EDP department. Its quality will greatly affect the short- and long-range performance of the department. One detriment of detailed methodology is that it leaves a psychological impression that success can be achieved by filling out forms. This will not work for planning. Evaluations must be thorough and complete, conclusions must be based on in-depth insight, and solutions and programs must be imaginative and creative.

The planning methodology, supported by all other techniques discussed, provides all the tools for effectively managing the EDP department. The last management consideration is establishing a comprehensive reporting system to measure the performance of the EDP department as a whole and evaluate how well all these techniques are working.

-10-

Measuring the EDP Function

Given the scope of activities of the EDP department, the director of data processing requires a comprehensive reporting system to ensure he is up to date on all activities. This chapter will identify the activities that should be measured on a continuous basis and provide sample report formats for each area. A philosophy of reporting will be discussed. Managers and professionals at all levels require information in order to perform their jobs. The needs of each vary in respect to format and the amount of detail required. The reporting system presented here is designed basically for the needs of the director of data processing. Modified reports may be required by others, but variations are too numerous to be covered here.

REPORTING PHILOSOPHY

Before proceeding with the design of formal reports, an important point of philosophy needs to be made. Management reports are intended to provide the director of data processing with complete information that can be digested quickly in his busy schedule. However, there is no substitute for going out into the department periodically and observing what really is happening. Many a manager has been surprised to encounter problems for which he thought there were adequate controls in place, but the problems existed because the procedures were not being used. It is so important that it is worth repeating: an occasional walk around the department not only is good for purposes of review, but is a sound practice from an employee relations viewpoint.

The reporting concept needs some analysis before we can deal with specific reporting areas and reports. Management reports should not be merely listings of statistics of one sort or another. For example, a listing of all instances of hardware failures in chronological order is of little value for management reporting purposes. The report may give a lot of information, but it doesn't tell much. Is the performance good or bad? What action is required? Are there any trends developing? Without considerable analysis on the reader's part, little value is obtained from information like this. Management reporting must take one of two formats: exception reporting or summary reporting.

Exception reports show deviations from some norm. Daily reporting of late report deliveries to users is an example of exception reporting. The report shows those outputs not delivered on schedule, rather than lists all scheduled shipments with the scheduled and actual times of each. This type of report highlights a specific problem area and indicates where action may be necessary.

The other type of management reporting is summary statistics, which depict the overall performance of an activity. To be effective, this type of report requires a basis of comparison, such as historical trends or standards, to put the data in perspective. More appropriate hardware-downtime reporting than just discussed might include a report showing the aggregate downtime for a particular device compared to an agreed-upon standard.

The frequency of reports varies according to their intended function. An exception report of late outputs, intended to highlight action required, is of little use if distributed weekly or monthly after the fact. Summary reporting of hardware failures designed to evaluate performance, on the other hand, is meaningless if the reporting period is too short.

Several reports have been discussed prior to this chapter, including the daily status report in the scheduling system and the EDP project status reports created by the project control system. These reports, as well as many others, will comprise a recommended set of management reports for top EDP management. For the sake of completeness, all reports will be shown in this chapter, even at the expense of repetition.

REPORTS ON THE EDP PLAN STATUS

If the EDP plan is the basic guide for the EDP department, then a management reporting system should begin with the plan before concerning itself with its details. Both the long-range and the operational portions of the plan should be monitored. Long-range-plan reviews are closely enough controlled by reviews during annual updating. However, the operational plan, because of its shorter span, requires review on a monthly basis. The measurable portions that should be addressed are objectives, projects, and budget. All sample reports that follow assume that the reporting period runs from January through December. Minor modifications would be required for a different fiscal period.

Figure 10-1 is a sample format of a status report on the objectives of the EDP plan. The organizational description information is completed at the top, and each objective within the approved plan is listed in the first column. Each month the actual result, in terms of the appropriate quantitative units, for each objective is listed. This shows the progress throughout the year toward the established objective.

Similarly, a summary report on the status of planned projects can be useful. Figure 10-2 is a format that serves this purpose. The report lists projects scheduled through the month of report. A status code is indicated for each one, such as N for "not started," B for "behind schedule," O for "on schedule," A for "ahead of schedule," and C for "project completed." The comments column is used to explain variances from plan. Additional detail is also needed and will be discussed later, but a summary of this sort is good for a quick review.

Two reports are necessary for budget control: one to show actual dollars spent as compared to budget as of a given point, and another to project the sum of incurred expenses and reestimated costs to the

163

Objective	Jan	Feb	Mar	Apr	May	Jun	Jul	Aug	Sep	Oct	Nov	Dec	Comments

Department_____

Group_____

Section_____

Figure 10-1.   EDP plan objectives: status report form.

Figure 10-2. Project status summary form.

Month of_____

PROJECT	STATUS	COMMENTS
Installment Loans	N	Not scheduled to begin until next month.
Purchasing Control	O	Expect to complete project by year end as scheduled.
Financial Control	B	User made major changes to specifications during pro-gramming phase.
DDA/Data Base System	B	Major technical problems encountered with data management. Software vendor has corrected problems. Expect to be back on schedule in two months.

total budget for the year. As discussed in relation to project control methods, merely comparing budget to actual expenses does not give a meaningful interim comparison, because there is no consideration of how much of the planned work has been completed. Therefore, another comparison is also required here. Each month the actual costs are noted for each expense category. Then the projected expenses for the remainder of the year are noted and the sum of the two compared against the original budget. In effect, the budget for the remaining months is reestimated and added to actual expenses.

Figures 10-3 and 10-4 show sample budget report forms. The reports for all three components of the plan—objectives, projects, and budget—should be prepared for the lowest organizational unit. This means that the reports should be additionally prepared at the shift and section levels and then consolidated upward, creating reports for each organizational level, including for the EDP department as a whole. This allows each management level to understand its performance in respect to its portion of the plan, and it enables the director of data processing to review the department as a whole and each of its components.

Figure 10-3. Sample EDP budget status report.

Month Ending

	Current			Year to Date		
Category	Budget	Expense	Variance	Budget	Expense	Variance
Payroll	246,000	248,000	(2,000)	492,000	488,000	4,000
Hardware	145,000	145,000	– 0 –	290,000	290,000	– 0 –
Purchased Software	– 0 –	– 0 –	– 0 –	10,000	12,000	(2,000)
Furniture/Equipment	12,000	13,000	(1,000)	24,000	28,000	(4,000)
Facility Allocation	18,000	17,000	1,000	36,000	32,000	4,000
Totals	421,000	423,000	(2,000)	852,000	850,000	2,000

Figure 10-4. Sample budget report: estimated costs to budget.

Month Ending

Expense	Costs to Date	Estimated to Year End	Budget	Variance
Payroll	488,000	2,685,000	2,952,000	267,000
Hardware	290,000	1,780,000	1,740,000	(40,000)
Purchased Software	12,000	12,000	10,000	(2,000)
Furniture/Equipment	28,000	152,000	144,000	(8,000)
Facility Allocation	32,000	203,000	216,000	13,000
Totals	850,000	4,832,000	5,062,000	230,000

166

MAJOR ACTIVITIES	STATUS	PROJECT PLAN 1977								1978												
	Original / Ahead / Revised	MAY	JUNE	JULY	AUG	SEPT	OCT	NOV	DEC	JAN	FEB	MAR	APRIL	MAY	JUNE	JULY	AUG	SEPT	OCT	NOV	DEC
Purchase Software																					
Acquire Interim Space																					
Recruit Personnel																					
Install S 370 115																					
Develop and Implement New Systems																					
Tenant Billing																					
TTC Billing																					
General Ledger																					
Payroll/Labor Dist.																					
Accounts Payable																					
Accounts Receivable																					
Job Cost (New)																					
Fixed Assets																					
Parallel two computers																					
Release H 2020																					

Figure 10-5. Summary project plan.

OTHER DEPARTMENTAL REPORTS

In the discussions of change management and problem control, certain information requirements were defined. The weekly EDP trouble recap (Figure 6-10) and problem history summary (Figure 6-11) found in Chapter 6 are intended to provide EDP management with comprehensive reporting in respect to problem situations. In order to carry out its responsibility of reviewing implementation schedules and regulating the rate of change, the EDP department must prepare a report of scheduled implementations. A chart as in Figure 10-5 is useful for this purpose. The chart is completed initially during the operational planning activity and is updated as needed for the weekly change management committee meeting.

A summary report of the findings of the EDP department self-audit should be prepared for the director of data processing on a monthly basis. The audit report should be accompanied by the responses from subordinate managers.

Although a project status summary report is prepared as part of the monthly plan analysis, the director of data processing should have more frequent and more detailed information on project status. The director should therefore be on the distribution list for the EDP

Figure 10-6. Daily teleprocessing status report.

Date

Application	Scheduled Hours	Hours Down	Percent Down-time	Cause of Downtime Hours			
				Hard-ware	Appli-cation	Soft-ware	Oper-ation
Customer Information	10	.3	3%	.3			
Financial Control	12	.5	4%	.3	.2		
Vehicle Scheduling	10	.3	3%	.3			
Totals	32	1.1	3%	.9	.2		

168

project status report (Figure 5-3). These reports should be prepared on a weekly basis. Again, a report should be prepared for each organizational unit. To avoid repetition, only the lowest level will report projects individually. The upward consolidation merely recaps group and department totals to show overall performance.

The director of data processing should review all feasibility studies of projects undertaken and approve the results. Especially in a larger shop, it is not possible for him to review all subsequent phases, but a review of at least the feasibility studies will ensure that he understands what is being done and why. For major projects, the director will find a management presentation of key phases valuable to assure that these are progressing appropriately.

SERVICE MEASUREMENTS

The computer services group requires additional important management reports. Customer service should be measured both on very short intervals and on a historical basis. The EDP daily status should be reviewed each day by the director of data processing so that he can keep abreast of any processing delays. For installations that have on-line applications, a daily report such as the one in Figure 10-6 will also be useful. If a director of data processing is not reviewing reports like these on a daily basis, he will eventually wish he had—at the latest when he is approached by an angry user or top management about a problem on which he has no information. A monthly report of teleprocessing downtime similar to Figure 10-6 should also be prepared. In addition, a simple graph showing monthly downtime quickly reflects long-range trends. The report in Figure 10-7 summarizes the monthly performance of delivering reports on schedule. Graphs showing long-range trends are also useful to complement such a report. Because the causes of late outputs are numerous and may need detailed analysis, a monthly report on the causes of late outputs is also required. Figure 10-8 suggests a format for this report. Totals in this report and in the monthly schedule performance report should, of course, agree.

Application	Total Shipments	Number Late	Percent Late

Figure 10-7.   Report on monthly schedule performance.

Cause	Total Occurrences	Percent of Total Late Outputs

Figure 10.8.   Monthly report on late outputs by cause.

				Device	
Month	Number	Hours Down	Percent	Standard Percent	Variance
January					
February					
March					
October					
November					
December					
Total					

Figure 10-9.   Hardware reliability report.

REPORTS ON HARDWARE STATUS

Reports on hardware malfunctions and other aspects of hardware should be prepared monthly, although the manager of computer services will clearly want more frequent reporting and should naturally apprise the director of data processing of any major problems. Figure 10-9 is a format for a monthly hardware report. One page is used for each device type. Terminal equipment should be included for teleprocessing users.

Utilization reports for hardware are possible, but, as earlier noted, summary statistics on hardware utilization are relatively meaningless and often misleading. The preferred approach is for the technical development group to issue a periodic report, with statistics, charts, graphs, and accompanying analysis, which thoughtfully presents the utilization picture and projects trends. Hardware orders are often numerous, especially in the larger shops. A monthly status report on hardware orders is a useful double-check for the director of data processing and others on what is scheduled for delivery. The form should be set up to list, in columns, the following information: Order Date, Vendor, Model Description, Quantity, Requested Date, Vendor Date, Ordered By. The "Requested Date" column shows when the EDP department desires delivery. "Vendor Date" is the vendor's current planned shipment date. These may not always be the same, and may highlight areas where scheduling problems need attention.

MISCELLANEOUS REPORTS

The preceding reports are the principal types required in the EDP department. There are a few additional areas that may call for reports. But this depends on the environment of each particular EDP department. Sometimes reports may be needed temporarily to highlight special situations. These should be discontinued when no longer needed. Reporting can be overdone. Design reports that provide useful information and can be quickly analyzed yet, in aggregate, provide a true picture of the performance of the EDP department.

171

-11-

Other EDP Management Issues

BESIDES consideration of the management techniques presented in this book, there are several miscellaneous issues that must be faced sooner or later by EDP managers. Decisions must be made on these issues, and eventually policies for dealing with them will be adopted by most EDP departments. The purpose of this chapter is to identify and discuss some of these issues in order to provide a basis for future decisions by EDP managers.

PURCHASED SOFTWARE PACKAGES

Packaged software has become an important factor in the EDP industry, and its use will probably increase in the future. There are software packages for many types of applications and special utility functions. They are sold by hardware vendors, software houses specializing in packaged software, and independent installations and individuals who are trying to recoup costs or make a profit on software developed for their own use. Some software packages are very good, and some are very bad. Some sellers provide valuable services, and others only marginal support. Packaged software can provide benefits to the user, but not in every instance, so its use must be carefully evaluated.

Packaged software potentially provides several advantages to the user. Cost is the most obvious benefit. Normally, the user cannot develop from scratch an application system for the cost of purchasing and installing a package. In case of tight schedule requirements, software packages may be preferable, since they normally can be installed more quickly than an in-house system. Potentially, a commercially sold software package offers a tried software system that will be more dependable in early operation.

With all these advantages, it would seem that an EDP manager couldn't go wrong. However, many software acquisitions turn out to be nightmares. Many conversions are disasters, schedule slippages are frequently incurred, and programming costs often turn out to be substantial. The EDP manager must understand the benefits and limitations of the packaged software approach and ensure that the investment is worthwhile.

Implementing Purchased Software

When implementing a software system, there is simply no substitute for a complete requirements study. Many users in the market for packaged software think they can short-cut the evaluation by having user departments review a potential package as an alternative to the requirements study. This inevitably leads to, at best, an evaluation of what the vendor package provides, without adequate comparison to what really is needed. Eventually, this leads to discovery of missing functions, which will require modifications or rewrites of the software or portions thereof.

Before entering the packaged software market, then, the EDP department must complete a detailed requirements study, just as if it were going to develop its own programs. If a package appears a possibility, then it must be evaluated against the detailed criteria established by the study. When performing this analysis, the EDP department must understand where the user might be flexible on the requirements. Certainly, no package will meet every requirement including report formats and so on, so some flexibility is required, or

173

the evaluation will never be fruitful. The end user must be sold on the benefits of a purchased package to him so that he will cooperate. He should understand that as soon as the company begins modifying the package here and there, some risk is inherent and some of the benefit is lost.

The requirements match is the most crucial part of evaluating packaged software, because herein lies the biggest disadvantage of the packaged software approach. The end user by definition will never get exactly what he needs, as he would—theoretically at least—when software is custom-designed for his needs. This is the price you pay for the advantages of packaged software.

Once a package is found that meets the requirements, the vendor or vendors must be researched. Before doing this, the extent of the support desired from the vendor must be defined. If the expectation is to buy a package, install it, and maintain it in-house with nominal vendor support, then vendor credentials are not that crucial. However, very often the buyer will desire substantial installation support and ongoing maintenance. And maintenance can be extremely valuable, because the user has not developed the in-house expertise he does when producing his own software. In this case, the business reputation of the vendor is vital.

Vendor investigations begin with the evaluation of the company. The general business position and financial standing are important. Talk to some current customers. Ask the vendor to produce a complete client list, or at least an extensive sample. Don't get caught by a vendor who will supply only a handful of references, because even a bad vendor can always somehow come up with a client who will provide a good reference. Talk to the references about the package, too.

The package review begins with the client references. Make sure the version vouched for is exactly the same as yours, not just another package doing the same functions. Some customers have been disappointed to find the package they purchased is a new system provided by the vendor, not the proven one they discussed with references. The documentation should be reviewed for completeness and usability. A technical evaluation must be performed to ensure that technically the package meets installation standards. Be cautious if the package has not been used in the exact hardware and software environment of the EDP department, because the "minor" changes required to make it fit can be troublesome.

Once a vendor has been selected, final negotiations take place. Price, especially with some of the smaller firms, is negotiable, so don't get out the checkbook too quickly. Vendors like to quote installation support in terms of man-days. This has pitfalls when tasks are not accomplished within the time anticipated. So try to get the vendor to agree on a price for completion of specific tasks such as compilation and installation rather than man-days. Many vendors prefer to base acceptance tests on their data. But too often these tests come out fine, and then the system falls apart when user data are entered. There has been at least one instance where a vendor has contrived test data to cover up a known bug in the system. Insist on a test with in-house data before funds are paid out unconditionally.

When all these activities are completed and the vendor has passed all tests, the EDP department will probably have a good experience. This discussion has highlighted problems, but is not intended to discourage package acquisition, because the benefits are real, nor to slight all the vendors in this business, as there are some excellent ones. The point is that the EDP department must understand the issues involved and take appropriate steps before signing contracts.

CONSULTANTS AND CONTRACT PROGRAMMERS

EDP departments as a whole are large users of outside consultants and contract personnel. There are many companies that specialize in providing these services, and the services can be very valuable if used properly. However, many EDP departments spend virtual fortunes and get little or nothing in return. To a large extent, they are victims of their own actions, because they don't know how to select outside support properly or how to utilize such people well once they are chosen.

For purposes of this discussion, a definition of contractors and consultants is required. They are not the same. Consultants are companies or individuals offering the organization their expertise in certain technologies or administrative or management techniques. Consultants usually are contracted to complete one or more specific projects, and they normally provide project management for their personnel. Consultant rates can vary from $50 to $150 per hour plus expenses. Contracting companies in the EDP business provide programming and analytical manpower for the customer. The customer supervises the people, and rates are generally $20 to $30 an hour.

One of the issues is understanding when each type of company is to be used. This is complicated by the fact that many contracting firms call themselves consultants, possibly misleading the customer as to what services they provide. There is an obvious dollar difference in the rates charged by each type of company; therefore, it is important to use the right type in the right situation. Basically, consultants are used when a special area of expertise is necessary or when a high degree of objectivity is required but not available in-house. Contract personnel companies are used to handle peak-load requirements of technical personnel. The roles are not normally interchangeable.

Using Consultants

Because consultants are asked to provide a tangible end product—an analysis or study—and they manage the development of the end product, selection of the right firm is more important than an evaluation of the individuals in it. The obvious exception to this is the very small firm of only one or a few persons, where ensuring that individual consultants have experience in the hiring company's industry and expertise in the particular area of study is important. Although individuals are not normally interviewed, it is useful to ask who will be assigned to the contemplated project and request a brief resume of each to ensure that experience is appropriate for the assignment. The "you pay while they learn" approach can make the project much more expensive.

Assignments should be for specific projects with a predefined end product to be delivered on a specified date. The director of data processing or somebody designated by him should act as a liaison so the consultants do not get conflicting direction. Many companies bring in consultants to do an overhaul when the EDP department collapses, but the trick is to avoid this situation.

Previously, several areas of consultants use have been noted, including development of performance appraisal systems, scheduling procedures, and planning methodologies. Another possible use is a comparative hardware analysis when internal organizational factors prevent an objective analysis in-house. The feasibility or planning study for a new technology such as data base management might be a beneficial consultant project if the EDP department has no expertise in the area.

There are numerous other types of projects where consultants can be used in a worthwhile manner. But manage this resource like any other. Make sure they are controlled and you obtain the most for the money. Avoid huge projects where the consultants are asked to manage and develop large computer systems and the like. If the organization needs consultants for these types of projects, it probably isn't ready for them anyway. Finally, don't let consultants become such a part of the operation that they find a permanent place. Some companies actually try to make work for established consultants who are aboard instead of letting requirements dictate their presence. Let them complete their assignments and get out.

Using Contract Programmers

Because contracting firms offer no services other than locating and providing personnel, the company itself is of relatively less importance. However, some companies provide better compensation and screen better, and therefore have a higher overall caliber of personnel. Some are more concerned with their general reputations and long-term business relationships and behave accordingly. On the other hand, a number of these firms are in business for a quick buck and behave consistent with this. So, there is a difference, and the company providing contract personnel should be investigated to some extent. But the most important consideration is the personnel. Contract programmers should be interviewed and their histories checked, nearly to the same extent as with employees to be hired. This is especially true for programmers considered for larger projects of a long duration. Don't rely on claims by the contracting company that the individual is one of their best. Contract personnel should be expected to have all the job qualifications of in-house personnel, to conform to installation rules, and to get results. If they don't, the company's obligation to them by definition is less than to department employees and they should be dismissed quickly. This point is made because many contract employees expect special considerations for some reason, and allowing this will do nothing but minimize the return on investment and cause morale problems.

Contract personnel are used to fill peak load requirements of programmers and analysts. This can result from unexpected systems activity or the inability of the department to hire staff at the desired levels. The additional expense certainly makes this arrangement unattractive in the long run as an alternative to in-house staffing. Contractors have the additional disadvantage of taking knowledge gained with them when they leave. Contract personnel should not be used to complete entire projects or to have major roles in a project. Turnover of contract personnel will be higher than with in-house personnel, so the risk must be minimized.

EDP CONTRACTS

Throughout, our discussions regarding various vendor relationships of the EDP department have emphasized the need to investigate the business reputation of the vendor being considered. Solutions negotiated and agreed to by businessmen are preferable to legal alternatives. If the job isn't done right by a vendor, the damage and disruption to the EDP department can never be completely compensated for. Litigation and other legal maneuvering is expensive and is normally not justifiable except in the largest contracts, even when the customer has clearly been harmed. However, there is always the possibility that the legal alternative may be required someday, so contracts should be drawn for every major vendor relationship, and the wording needs more than casual consideration. The contract can be an informal letter outlining the agreement, or it can be a formal legal document. This depends upon the vendor and the financial commitment contemplated.

Before getting into contracts, get the advice of a competent attorney with some experience in EDP contracts. He or she should provide legal counsel regarding all aspects of the contract. With the exception of a handful of the very largest of EDP vendors, contract terms and wording are normally negotiable to some extent, so efforts in contract reviews can be worthwhile. The following are some general considerations relative to contracts, although the presentation does not purport to be a comprehensive guideline for contract drafting.

As a buyer, the EDP department is vitally interested in four aspects of the contract. First, there must be a precise definition of what goods and services are to be provided. Second, the contract must specify the guarantees and warranties provided for the products and specifications. Third, the contract should specify what recourses the buyer has and what the penalties are for not meeting the specifications. Finally, the criteria and terms for use of the product by the user must be spelled out.

Too often EDP contracts only specify a product name or give a general description of the product. Detailed specifications of the product, though usually contained in sales material, are often not included as part of the contract. The user subsequently finds that the product does not meet his needs, but memories are vague regarding verbal discussions and commitments, so the user has little recourse if the seller does not respond in good faith. Contracts should include a detailed description of the product or service which includes all elements vital to the EDP department. For example, if a software package is being purchased, the specifications should include a description of the functions to be provided, the detail of the technical environment the software will operate in, and any other critical items. The objective is to ensure that the product will do, *in the buyer's environment,* what the buyer anticipates. For general-purpose products, the seller cannot necessarily guarantee that the product will do everything the user wants, because the seller doesn't totally understand the user environment, but the seller should be willing to document his claims. If the seller is notified early that he will be required to do this, the buyer may achieve the added advantage of stifling marketing rhetoric of meaningless claims.

The seller will—with justification in some cases—probably try to include a paragraph in which the buyer waives warranties or

179

guarantees. These waivers are often found in a paragraph called Limitation of Liability. In effect, the seller will say that he will attempt to resolve any problems encountered to the extent of his ability, but that he makes no other warranties. This leaves the buyer with dubious recourse if the product doesn't perform. The seller must protect himself to some degree, but he should not be allowed to totally abdicate responsibility for nonperformance. Contract law provides for certain implied warranties that can be significant. Waiving implied warranties should not be done without thought. The buyer should understand his rights and, in consultation with his attorney, determine the minumum warranty acceptable. Reason must prevail. If the buyer makes excessive demands, no one will want to do business. On the other hand, if the seller is unwilling to make reasonable guarantees, the buyer should be suspicious and assume that the seller may have something to hide.

Closely related to the issue of warranties is that of the seller's liability for not meeting specified requirements. The common practice is for the vendor to specify that his liability is not to exceed the purchase price or rental payments for the product or service. Some businesses, such as contract programming companies, don't even offer that much. They rent personnel and get payment, regardless of performance. However, after the buyer has spent substantial sums installing a product that doesn't live up to vendor claims, the return of the purchase price may not even begin to compensate for losses.

Vendors must protect themselves from multimillion-dollar lawsuits based on losses from consequential damages such as loss of business opportunity. But it is not unreasonable to expect compensation for direct incidental costs such as manpower invested. One reasonable approach is to specify a limit that protects the vendor from absurd claims and still allows the user some recourse such as two or three times the purchase price. Maybe qualifying circumstances for claims, such as damages resulting from vendor misrepresentation or neglect, will be required.

The seller will propose several types of restrictions on the use of the product by the customer. Some of these, like guarantees by the user that he will keep confidential the proprietary information supplied by the seller, are reasonable. Others may not be as reasonable. The buyer must understand how he wants to use the product and ensure that the contract does not prevent him from doing so.

Contracts with contract programming companies are a little different, because these companies offer no real product or service other than providing manpower. Because contract programming companies do not supervise their people, they cannot be totally liable for the work done. Nonetheless, there are a few things the EDP department can do to prevent the vendor from being totally off the hook and to discourage him from sending just anyone.

The standard argument by marketing personnel is that the customer is protected by the company's need to protect its long-term business reputation. This, unfortunately, is a lot of malarkey. There are some businesses of this type that have a long-range perspective, but all too many are driven by short-term considerations. The first step the EDP department can take is to require a trial period to determine if the contractor actually has the alleged qualifications. If he doesn't live up, his services can be terminated with no billings at all made to the customer. Many contracting companies will provide this stipulation, but they like to limit the time period to the first week or less. This is just not enough time to evaluate the work, so get a 30-day guarantee. Because the turnover is expected to be high, the contracting company should be required to underwrite some of the costs of turnover by its people that causes rework. A good way to do this is to require a credit of two weeks or so, which is used to cover the cost of orientation for replacement personnel.

The contract terms suggested here will provide advantages to the EDP department. Not only does the appropriate contract provide legal recourse, but the existence of the recourse will be additional motivation for the vendor to make every effort to live up to commitments. Thus a good contract may head off problems that may otherwise have been encountered. And this is of course the primary objective: to receive what was anticipated. The EDP manager should understand that his vendors, even the good ones, may not accept everything dictated by the customer. If the product is highly desirable, business requirements may necessitate compromises. These decisions should be evaluated on the basis of the risks and guided by considerations of overall needs.

ASSIMILATING TECHNOLOGICAL CHANGE

Another issue EDP managers must deal with is the constant offerings of new products, technologies, and systems concepts. Vendors can keep the managers of EDP departments busy on a full-time basis with proposals and sales meetings, if they are allowed to. Some of these new offerings can provide substantial benefits, and a few offer dramatic opportunities. No EDP manager can afford to ignore the new products if he is to continue to maximize progress toward goals: However, embracing technology for technology's sake will lead the EDP department away from its pronounced direction. The director of data processing must ensure that new opportunities are exploited, but at the same time ensure that business objectives are never subordinated to technology.

The biggest threat of technological improvement is that it may force the EDP department into a react mode. The EDP department has painstakingly developed its plan. Suddenly, a vendor appears with a new product with unheard-of price/performance advantages. The salesman, motivated by quotas for the new product, insists that the department cannot afford to wait. So, a new project is started to investigate and maybe install this wonder. But what has happened in the meantime to the plan? This somewhat sarcastic scenario takes place day after day in EDP departments. If it happens often enough, the department becomes disorganized.

Occasionally, an announcement may be so dramatic that it does in fact require some immediate attention. Once in a while a new product may be discovered which, although not in the original plan, is consistent with the current objectives. Herein lies the key to decisions. The business objectives of the EDP department are the driving force. The plan supports the objectives, so the disruptions to the plan threaten achievement of the objectives. Therefore, new announcements must be evaluated in this light. Do the products contribute to achievement of current objectives? Each new product must be screened and either rejected or postponed until a later time if it is not consistent with current objectives.

Another aspect of the rate of technological change is the attitude of EDP departments toward new technologies. Some EDP managers are inclined to use the latest technology and pride themselves on being on the leading edge. Others resist changes until absolutely forced to. The practical approach is somewhere in between.

Again, this issue must be resolved with a view to business objectives. The old EDP saying that "pioneers wind up with arrows" is still true. As an industry, EDP companies have not yet learned how to consistently develop new hardware and software products and debug them thoroughly before delivering them to the customer in the field. Despite often rigorous testing, the innumerable variables in the customer environment are just not yet repeated in the testing environment. The EDP manager who is the first with anything must expect an inordinate amount of problems, sometimes reaching a devastating level. However, holding steadfast to proven technology does not allow the EDP department to maximize opportunities and in the long run will create unanticipated problems.

The astute EDP manager will adopt a medium-ground policy. He will never be the first with new products. He understands that their promise and potential can be totally invalidated if implementation proves to be disastrous. He will even encourage his users to delay new applications that require substantially new products. On the other hand, he will ensure that his plans duly reflect opportunities in state-of-the-art technology.

MANAGEMENT AND CHANGE

The concepts presented in this book have been tested in practice. They are proven management techniques. An EDP manager who makes proper use of these techniques is assured of a high degree of success. However, the management approach advocated here is based on today's typical EDP environment. This environment has changed substantially from years past and will continue to evolve in the future. Approaches that are valid today may be obsolete tomorrow. As technology changes, so must management techniques. Certain concepts such as project management are virtually timeless. On the other hand, organization structure is designed for a specific situation and must change as circumstances do. Scheduling and control techniques must be kept compatible with the changing technology in which they operate. Even planning is affected, since the duration of the plan depends to a large degree on the environment.

The successful EDP manager will be cognizant of management changes as well as technological changes. He will perceive the difference in requirements for EDP employees, have insight into shifting responsibilities, and act where necessary to replace or update management methods. The top EDP manager will anticipate the need for change and adapt, not wait for poor performance of his department to dictate it. For the goal is not merely to establish an effective EDP organization, but to maintain one.

-12-

Strictly Personal

Chapter 11 concluded the presentation of EDP management techniques. This chapter is only indirectly related to the main topic and is, therefore, optional reading. Its intent is to offer some personal observations on techniques and philosophies that may be relevant to EDP managers. The primary target is the director of data processing, but points made should be of interest to other EDP managers.

ABOUT PEOPLE

Chapter 7 discussed techniques for managing personnel resources. Some managers would tend to conclude that designing an employment package along the lines recommended will be sufficient to ensure good employee relations. But here again, blind adherence to formal methods can be dangerous. People are obviously different from any other resource. Unlike the procedure with a computer, simply entering the right input does not necessarily ensure the desired output. People have a wide variety of emotions, desires, and anxieties that affect their interaction in the work environment. This is not an argument against the techniques presented in Chapter 7, merely a statement that these alone just simply are not enough.

The successful manager will take the time—or make the time, if he has to—to relate to his people on matters other than production statistics and project status. The manager must understand the employee's feeling about his position—how well it meets his personal needs and career aspirations, and what problems the employment relationship presents for him. Going a step further, showing an interest in personal problems of the employee will solidify the relationship. This is not to suggest the manager become a guidance counselor; but some support during a personal crisis may never be forgotten.

I'm not about to suggest another checklist of do's and dont's for the manager. Contrived interest will be easily recognized and could well have a negative effect. This is a matter of philosophy. Given that companies are people, there must be more to their purpose than profits. If philosophical arguments are not enough motivation for the manager to take time with his people, then certainly all the practical arguments about production levels and turnover rates should be. In any case, the successful manager will understand the importance of taking an interest in his people. He will also choose subordinate managers who are also sincerely interested in the well-being of the staff.

Satisfying these requirements demands more than a periodic meeting or a so-called "open door policy." It is a matter of day-to-day behavior. Checking on an employee recently absent because of illness, inquiring about the new baby, or asking how the employee is settling in his new house—that is the kind of behavior that creates good feelings. Expressions of sympathy when an employee calls to report an absence due to a death in the family, rather than a volley of questions about the duration of the absence and the status of job assignments, will build good relationships. Sincerely trying to understand how the job environment could better serve individual employee aspirations, and taking reasonable actions accordingly, will enhance the employee's attitude toward the company. Examples are endless.

Managing people is really what the job is all about. There is no manager too busy and no schedule too tight to justify not carrying out that responsibility. Think about it! Attitudes here can make significant contributions to success and failure, as well as to the satisfaction the manager himself gets from his job.

186

Seminars in motivation theory and behavior can be beneficial to the thoughtful manager who values the welfare of employees. Sending managers without concern for people to seminars is no more effective than "putting perfume on a pig." No matter how bright these people might be, they should be weeded out of the management ranks.

HABITS OF THE EDP DIRECTOR

The need for organization, structure, and a planned approach to EDP management has been stressed throughout this book. The role of the director of data processing as a moving force in the organization has been noted. What may not be as apparent is the impact that the personal habits of the director of data processing have on the overall character of his organization. The manager who becomes so engrossed in the detail of a few isolated problems will lose control of his organization. The plan will not be properly developed without him, nor will it be properly executed without his direction. An EDP manager who reacts to daily circumstances rather than in accordance with a strategy will affect his organization in the same way. The director who bypasses organization channels and personally directs the activities at various levels will lose the advantage of any organization structure.

In essence, the director must behave in a manner consistent with the intent of those management techniques that he wants the department to use. The director of data processing, in the real sense of the word, is a manager and not a doer. He is primarily concerned with developing the plan, monitoring its status, directing the solution of problems, and generally ensuring completion of the plan.

Personal Organization

Because of the number of decisions and activities to follow up on, the director of data processing must have a finely tuned sense of personal organization. He must have the ability to review an issue, make a decision, direct accordingly, and follow up on the execution at the proper time. He does not want to direct action to be taken and forget about it, but he cannot afford to stack his desk with pending items. A very simple but priceless tool for a busy manager is the use of a personal "tickler" or followup file. The file is usually maintained by a personal secretary. The followup file has a set of folders, numbered 1 through 31 for each day of the month. As items are noted for followup at a later date, a note is placed in the file indicating the month, date, and even year it is to be subsequently reviewed. The item is filed according to date. Each day, the items for the date are pulled for that day's attention.

Just as the director of data processing cannot be too involved in details of the operation, he mustn't become too divorced from the overall operation either. He must make conscious decisions regarding allocation of his time. He must budget his time between subordinates, superior, users, vendors, and others. This requires reasonably rigid scheduling. He cannot afford to allow the operation to become bogged down awaiting his review and decisions; on the other hand, he cannot allow his schedule to be constantly disrupted because of the lack of discipline of others. Meeting schedules should be planned in advance and adhered to, although the schedule should not be so tight as to exclude attention to unexpected problems which can arise.

A good habit to get into is to have a weekly meeting with each direct subordinate. These should be structured as one-on-one meetings, with the agenda loosely defined as a review of progress to the plan, discussion of problem areas, and any other matter of significance. This ensures that the director constantly stays in touch with all areas of the department, even when he may be preoccupied with a particular activity. It also provides an opportunity to handle a number of small matters at one time, and thus avoids a continuous flood of small meetings. And it is a good way to keep in touch with each subordinate on a personal basis.

Allegiance Is Ultimately to the Owners

Other philosophies and attitudes of the director of data processing will also have substantial impact on the performance of the EDP department. The director is, and should perceive himself as, an important part of the company management team. His primary allegiance must be to the business objectives of the company. As a member of the team, he has the right and even the obligation to present his ideas on these objectives. However, the final determination of these objectives is up to the owners of the business and their appointed representatives. The director of data processing is responsible for directing his organization in accordance with these objectives, even if they are not consistent with his wishes or personal beliefs. To do other than this is presuming that he knows more about what the owners want than the owners themselves, and he can only misdirect the EDP department in this mode.

The objective of this philosophy is not to muffle dissent. Certainly, all managers must try to defend their convictions, but there is sometimes a fine line between living up to professional responsibilities and being plain stubborn.

Careers and Risk

The director of data processing must consciously evaluate another factor that affects his behavior. There are many occasions where a director must face decisions that force him, to some degree, to choose between personal objectives and the performance of the EDP department. For example, when the department's objectives are set, a subtle choice may sometimes be made between setting objectives that can easily be achieved or ones that are reasonable but require a real effort to produce results. The former approach is safer, because the director will be "successful" according to less demanding criteria, whereas the latter approach is riskier, but has the potential for even higher achievement. Essentially a manager will adopt one of two underlying approaches. He will decide either to do what *appears* to be a good job, or to try to do what really *is* a good job. Every manager probably does a little of both in a specific situation, but most tend to lean one way or the other the preponderance of time. This conflict arises in many situations. Should the influential head of another department be challenged when he is clearly wrong in respect to the business objectives? Is a new program with tremendous potential overlooked if there is an unknown aspect and, therefore, a possibility of failure? Should action be taken in regard to an incompetent subordinate who has connections? Should a vendor be challenged when necessary if the company has a good relationship with top management?

The philosophy will make a big difference in the many difficult decisions made. The talented manager whose primary motivation is maximizing the performance of his area of responsibility will not only serve his company best in the long run, but will also serve himself as well. Perhaps it is naive, but I believe that those who behave otherwise and rely on politically related schemes to advance their careers will eventually be held accountable for their actions. If this were not true, there would be little hope for maximizing progress.

Index